SALT & SILVER
LATIN AMERICA

JOHANNES RIFFELMACHER

THOMAS KOSIKOWSKI

**Andrews McMeel
Publishing**®

a division of Andrews McMeel Universal

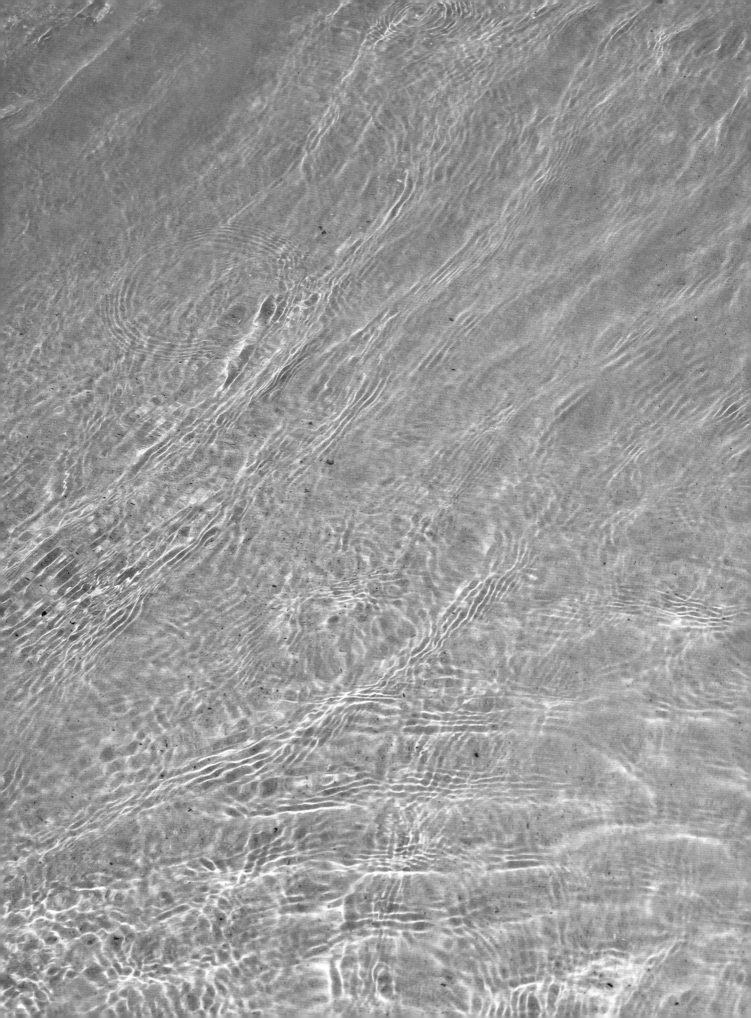

DEDICATED TO OUR FAMILIES

WE'D LIKE TO THANK THE FOLLOWING PEOPLE FOR THEIR SUPPORT:

Gabriel Lagos, Jana Federov, Tobias Szabo, Florian Kleinschmidt, Kim Schröder, Antine Yzer, Nils Poppe, Dominik Gauly, Yulia Morozova, Paul Pack, Thomas Güthaus, Mara Weber, Lars Bühlhoff, Laura Reil, Alexandra Reiner, Blue Tomato, Jan Traupe, Christoph Zingelmann, Florian Laudon, Andre Gießelmann, Daniela Garreton, Moisés Jiménez, Tania Maia, Erick Cuevas, Chris Bailey, Valeria Saenz, Linda Gondorf, Isa, Yojani, Frank, Rafa, Miles Jackson, Marcos, Fabian Wolf, Kingdrips, Dave Paco, Dan Landes, Jade Cicco, Blondy, Luigi, Pablo, Dess, Pauly, Charlie and Tony, Memo, Diego, Flor, EYOS, VRS, ALM, Alberto Hidalgo Aladzeme (aka "Don Beto"), Claudio Galdames, Fabio Andre Huerta Macuer, Raúl Cabrera, Edwin, Segundo, Jean Paul and the Naudón family, Volker Denks, Ka Shim, and Janni Schulte.

In January 2014, after over a year of planning, two guys from Hamburg set out to see the world. They quit their jobs, pooled all their savings, and off they went. Their baggage: two surfboards, a sharp knife, board shorts, and a backpack full of photo equipment. Their mission: to seek out the best waves and recipes in Latin America and compile them into a travel-surf cookbook. They spent a year on the road, starting in Cuba and moving down the Pacific coast of Mexico to Patagonia at the very tip of the continent.

You're holding the results in your hands: our book!

What awaits you here? All sorts of recipes for Latin American street and soul food as well as new inventions and tricks inspired by the local cuisines of the countries we visited that you can fill up on during your surf trip, even without a kitchen on the beach. Every surfer knows how important it is to stay fit and stick to a balanced diet. There's nothing more frustrating than having to leave the water early because you've run out of energy or strength. At the same time, as a surfer your constant pursuit of the perfect wave brings you into contact with countless exotic specialties that you never again want to do without. So it's a real bonus when, in addition to buying these new discoveries on the street, you can also cook them yourself at home.

In the course of our travels, we met talented surfers from Latin America and around the world who showed us the best surf spots, some of which we might never have found on our own. In our surf guides, we let these friends tell you about their favorite waves and beaches in their own voices, so you can learn about the best surf spots firsthand. All these spots are located along the Pacific and Caribbean coasts.

Finally, you'll read some great stories about the types of adventures you're bound to have if you spend a year sticking your curious nose into the business of armed Mexican guards or waves that are much too big for you. Enjoy the ride!

COZY & JO

TWO OLD FRIENDS. COZY IS THE PHOTOGRAPHER; JO IS THE ART DIRECTOR. BOTH ARE STREET-FOOD LOVERS AND SURFERS WHO ARE ALWAYS ON THE LOOKOUT FOR THE GOOD THINGS IN LIFE. JO WRITES; COZY TAKES PICTURES.

MEXICO
Cuba
Nicaragua
Costa Rica
Panama
Ecuador
Galápagos
Peru
Chile

CONTENTS

TRAVEL

WHERE TO?

Our original plan was a complete world tour, carrying everything with us, from Europe and Africa to Asia and Australia, and finally ending in South America. But we figured out pretty quickly that, among other things, this was going to cost us a bundle! The more we thought about it, the more we became convinced that for this type of project to succeed, we needed to explore the individual regions in depth, immerse ourselves deeply in the particular lifestyle and culture, find friends, and build relationships with locals—things that can't be done in a week.

We wanted to be more than just tourists. So instead of conquering the world, we chose eight countries in Central and South America, and we never found any reason to regret our decision. Maybe the greatest advantage of Latin America—apart from the thousands and thousands of miles of surfable Pacific coastline, innumerable tropical paradises, and cuisine that until now has been underrepresented in Europe and the United States—is the language. Spanish! Where else could you find an entire continent speaking the same language? (OK, in Brazil they speak Portuguese, but that country wasn't on our itinerary.) Financially, we were also drawn to Latin America by the cheap bus connections that made it possible for us to get around. Cars were also doable. So, Latin America it was!

"HOLA, HERMANO. TENEMOS HAMBRE. SABES DONDE HAY ALGO BUENO A COMER?"

For us, a knowledge of the language made all the difference. The trip wouldn't have been nearly as good if we hadn't learned to understand and speak Spanish. This became clear as soon as we got to Cuba, where there was only one person in the entire surfer and skater community who spoke English. In the beginning we knew only a few phrases in broken Spanish. For the first two months, our conversations were limited to fragments of words, and instead of speaking in whole sentences, we communicated with our hands and feet. But you can't let

small communication problems get in your way. Nobody's offended if you haven't yet mastered their native language. On the contrary, as soon as you try to communicate with the inhabitants in their own language, they treat you like you're part of a giant pan-American family. From Cuba to Chile, we never would have come into contact with so many fantastic people, places, and cuisines if we hadn't made the effort to learn the language.

Nobody expects you to be fluent in the language of every country you vacation in. But here's an experiment: Next time you're flying to another country, try learning the fifty most important phrases and words in that country's language. If you greet the taxi driver, thank the woman at the market, or ask for directions on the street in the local language, people will treat you differently. They'll be friendlier, and you might even pick up a few secret tips. But in any case, you're sure to find friendly faces.

ALWAYS BE OPEN

We've found in our encounters with foreign cultures that the most important thing is openness. It's our experience that the only way to really get to know and love a country is by disconnecting from the comfortable tourist network and forging your own path. It's better to stay in tiny private accommodations than in a hotel; better to go to the market and try out some bizarre but dirt-cheap and exotic treats than to eat the same old international dishes in mediocre tourist traps; better to go out in a boat with local fishermen than to book an expensive whale-watching tour; better to hitch a ride in the back of a pickup than to sip a cola on a luxury bus. But remember one thing:

TAKE CARE OF YOURSELF!

Clearly, anytime you travel abroad you need to be a little careful, but that doesn't mean you can't have adventures. The best way to assess a situation is to follow your gut instinct. If you're careful, if you don't carry your camera and valuables in plain sight and don't keep a fat wallet in your pants pocket, you should be OK. You're bound to run into a little bad luck, but even in extreme cases it's usually just a matter of money and a few valuables. Fortunately, we were never victims of a robbery or break-in, maybe because we took our cues from the behavior of the people around us. We ate where the locals ate, slept where the locals slept. We didn't wear expensive watches or carry around cameras in neighborhoods where even the Latinos held onto their wallets with both hands.

In a Mexican bar, Jo's wallet was stolen along with all his credit cards, but it showed up again a few days later, after our new local friends did some sniffing around. Also in Mexico, a mechanic to whom we'd given $500 to fix our car spent it on crack and crystal meth instead of our vehicle. But that's the worst that happened to us. Unfortunately, corrupt cops can be found everywhere, always the same creepy characters. In almost every country we visited, we were stopped for supposed "traffic violations." Sometimes we got away with a few friendly but pointed Spanish phrases; sometimes there was nothing to do but pay a cash "fine" to get our drivers' licenses back. Still, in some parts of Berlin your chances of being pulled over are almost as high as in Latin America. Having to take reasonable precautions shouldn't stop you from exploring the world. We found Latinos to be a very open and friendly people, and one or two dirty cops didn't change our opinion.

12

COOK

All our cooking skills are born out of passion and curiosity. Neither of us has had any professional culinary training. We like to wander through markets, greedily snap up anything that looks fresh and delicious, and then stand in the kitchen for hours turning these ingredients into new dishes. We got our basic knowledge from cookbooks, blogs, magazines, and videos. Strictly speaking, we were taught to cook by our mothers and fathers when we were little, and we've been building on that knowledge ever since.

Over time we've developed our own style as well as an awareness of what cooking and eating are all about. We're not the types to preach, but we are very critical of contemporary consumer behavior. So what you have here is really just our own opinions about cooking, life, and all the rest.

TWO PIRANHA FILLETS, PLEASE

Almost everything you need for the Latin American recipes in this book is available in Europe and the United States. In the case of a few exotic exceptions, such as grilled piranha in a sour jungle fruit sauce, we suggest alternative fishes and fruits that suit the dish just as well. What makes Latin American cuisine so special—as you'll see— is most often the method of preparation and what is for us the unusual combination of ingredients.

Sometimes the ingredients in the photos differ slightly from the ingredients in the recipes. That's because we weren't always able to find each of the ingredients we wanted on deserted Mexican beaches or in tiny Ecuadorian villages, when we took the photos, so we improvised. Often it can be easier to find typical Latin American ingredients in Europe and the United States than in a Nicaraguan fishing village. When we adapted the recipes to the ingredients available in Europe and the United States, and we didn't have an ingredient from the original recipe, we improvised again and replaced it with something else—all in the name of good flavor.

SURF

For each country we visited, we compiled a mini guide to the best spots that we surfed. Recently several highly professional, international guides to surf spots have been published. Our own tips serve to augment these guides with personal experience and, therefore, should be seen as nothing more nor less than highly subjective takes on some damn good waves. Our selection of surf spots ranges from beginner beach breaks to perfect barrels over razor-sharp reefs, so there should be something for everyone. But if what you want is 66-foot (20-meter) offshore Chilean reef waves, you'll be better off looking elsewhere. In this book you'll find plenty of bombs, from Cuba's urban surf spots to Galápagos point breaks and world-class Mexican barrels. To help you locate them, we've provided GPS coordinates. At several spots, we met surfers who knew the area like the back of their hand, and we were able to persuade some of them to share their knowledge with us. You'll find these tips in the relevant chapters.

WE CONSUME RESPECTFULLY

Mainly we respect the animals who give their lives for our meals, but we also respect the crooked cucumber, the apple with one small rotten part, and the farmer who can't afford to sell her free-range chickens at supermarket prices. We respect endangered fish species, cultural differences between the countries we live in and travel in, and the environment that surrounds us.

"Support your local business" is a goal worth pursuing. As you know, it's better to buy your muesli from the mom-and-pop store on the corner than to buy industrial oats from a supermarket. When we travel, we look for fresh, local products bought directly from the dealer and process them ourselves. But even in our home country, we do our best to develop product awareness. We'd rather go to an organic farmers' market once a week than stock up on provisions from a supermarket. We buy our meat from a butcher we trust and, ever since our stay in a vegan-vegetarian hostel (see page 123) and our *pachamanca* experience in Peru (see page 278), we also make it a point to have at least a couple of meatless days a week.

OUR FOOD IS AUTHENTIC

The food photos in this book were taken on the spot, literally on the way from the stove to the table or into our mouths. When it wasn't possible to take a picture—for example, when it was too dark—we skipped the photo and later cooked and photographed the same dish in Germany. Even in these cases, we were careful not to cheat or dress it up. So what you see in the photos is exactly what we cooked and ate. Our dishes don't always look as perfect as they do in regular cookbooks, but that's life. What matters is how they taste.

HOW HOT?

Especially when it comes to Latin American cuisine and your love of chile peppers, it's a matter of personal preference, and all the more because each chile pepper has its own, not always predictable, degree of spiciness. Personally, we love feeling like our mouths are on fire, but if you're not sure that the Aguachile (page 104) really needs three extremely hot green chiles, use only one or two and add half a green bell pepper instead. You also need to consult your own tastes with regard to garlic and salt. Consider our amounts to be guidelines, and don't be afraid to subtract or add an ingredient or two.

YOU DON'T NEED MUCH TO COOK

Most of the dishes in this book were prepared in poorly equipped hostel kitchens, over a beach fire, in the jungle, or in some private shack. But there are a few items that you'll really miss if you don't have them:

- SHARP KNIFE
- LARGE CUTTING BOARD
- MORTAR AND PESTLE
- BLENDER
- POT
- PAN
- LARGE BOWL

To give you an idea of what you can expect from each dish, we've divided the recipes into several categories:

LOW BUDGET — NO CASH? WE'VE ALL BEEN THERE. THE INGREDIENTS FOR RECIPES WITH THIS SYMBOL WON'T COST YOU A LOT OF MONEY.

VEGGIE — YOU DON'T ALWAYS HAVE TO EAT MEAT OR FISH. ONCE IN A WHILE, TREAT YOURSELF TO A PLATEFUL OF VEGETABLES!

BEACH FOOD — HAS YOUR SURF TRIP TAKEN YOU TO THE MIDDLE OF NOWHERE? NO PROBLEM! THESE RECIPES DON'T REQUIRE A KITCHEN.

FAST FOOD — AFTER SURFING, YOU'RE HUNGRY AND NOT IN THE MOOD TO SPEND TWO HOURS IN THE KITCHEN. TREAT YOURSELF TO SOMETHING FAST!

SLOW FOOD — MOST OF THE RECIPES IN THIS BOOK ARE FOR PEOPLE WHO LIKE TO COOK AND TAKE THE TIME TO DO IT. YOU'LL RECOGNIZE THEM BY THIS SYMBOL.

13

SEE VIDEO:

A trip to Cuba feels like a trip into the past. Because of the U.S. trade embargo, the range of products available is extremely limited, so in many regions you may feel like you've landed in the 1950s. Nevertheless, there's been a transformation over the past few years and we think the country's going to be changing rapidly. Large Western corporations are slowly penetrating the Cuban market, embargo or not. So our advice to you is: If you're thinking of visiting Cuba…do it NOW!

The island itself is a fairy-tale Caribbean paradise: crystal-clear water, snow-white sandy beaches, coconut palms—the whole package. But that wasn't what we were there for. Right from the start, we found something in Havana that interested us much more than the usual tourist fare—we joined up with a clique of Cuban skaters, surfers, and tattoo and graffiti artists. Life with this crowd was so exciting and varied that we made the executive decision to spend our entire Cuba trip in Havana. Instead of spending a month traveling around the country as we'd originally planned, we stayed the entire two months in Havana—interrupted only by a five-day excursion to Varadero, but that can be summed up in just a few words: palm trees, white beach, cheap mojitos, and tons of tourists.

Join us on our visit to Havana and go see the rest of Cuba firsthand on your next vacation.

El Bajo
Malecon

Playa Setenta

El Cayo

La sociedad

HAVANA

At the Frankfurt airport, we spent our last euros on greasy bratwurst and German pilsner in plastic cups. That this was not our most brilliant move became clear when, after an eleven-hour flight, we finally landed at the Havana airport and found ourselves planted in front of the only ATM, which had a display reading "out of order."

Barely arrived and already stranded. How would we get to the city? Nothing to do but hang out in the airport parking lot with a sheepish look and hope for a small miracle. We waited next to a line of ancient cars that would normally be seen only in gangster movies. But fate was looking out for us after all: After no more than five minutes, we were approached by Ka, a Hawaiian photographer. He, too, had just landed in Havana, and asked us if we wanted to share a cab into the city. We described our desperate financial position, and he offered to give us a lift. So we hailed one of the gangster cabs and took off.

In the center of Havana, we came up against our next obstacle: finding a place to sleep. In Cuba, it's common for tourists to stay in *casas particulares*, which are small rooms or mini apartments rented out by private citizens at prices regulated by the government. There's one on practically every street corner, and a night's lodging costs something between 14 and 28 euros. On the off chance that there might be a place for us, we rode with Ka to the *casa* he'd reserved in advance and hit the jackpot—the last available bunk bed for 4.50 euros each.

We spent the entire next day not withdrawing cash. All the ATMs conspired against us and our credit cards. But we didn't give up the search; we kept asking around and were sent from one place to another until we'd covered half the city. Still no go. With Ka's last $3, we ordered mojitos and Cuban cigars in a small bar. Why not? Helpless and frustrated, we chewed on our cigars and slowly worked our way through our drinks, staring out the door into the street, wondering where we'd be spending the night. Suddenly, Cozy's jaw dropped. He stared in disbelief as Michael Mackrodt, a German pro skater and Cozy's friend, walked in the door. Michael was as surprised to see us as we were to see him. He had a small skate and film crew in tow and was producing a new skate video. What a coincidence!

Everything went unbelievably smoothly after that. The guys had already found out where there were working ATMs, and they opened other doors for us, too. Within the next few days, we met Miles Jackson of Cuba Skate and, through one twisted connection after another, Havana's entire skate, surf, tattoo, and graffiti community. The clique called itself 23yG after the intersection nearest their favorite street skate spots. They were there every day, of course, so there was no need to schedule a meeting. Day and night we skated with the 23yG gang through Havana—through the streets by day, through the bars by night. Incidentally, here's a tip in case you run into financial trouble: The best places to get cash in Havana are the large luxury hotels, such as the Habana Libre. They usually have a *casa de cambios* where you can withdraw money with just a MasterCard and your passport. If you're on a tight budget, exchange your CUCs (Cuban Convertible Pesos) for *moneda nacional*, the parallel currency, and use the locals' infrastructure. You'll be able to ride from one end of the city to the other for just a few cents instead of a few dollars.

After skate sessions with 23yG, we often went to eat at an out-of-the-way courtyard restaurant, Mama Patio. To get there you have to pass through a maze of alleyways, dog kennels, and fire escape ladders until you finally reach a small balcony with palm trees belonging to a warm and friendly woman with the best soul food in Havana. You'll find Mama Patio in the Vedado quarter on Avenida 23 between Calles C and D. Our favorite dish was ropa vieja, or "old cloths," a traditional Cuban beef dish. According to tradition, this recipe has to be passed down from generation to generation. We got it from our friend and future chef Rafa, who got it from his grandmother. Check it out.

ROPA VIEJA
PULLED BEEF WITH RICE AND BLACK BEANS

Ropa vieja is served with rice or, to be exact: *moros y cristianos.* More about that on the next page. You could also serve this with deep-fried plantains.

SERVES 4

MARINADE

4 CUPS (1 L) MALT BEER
2 TABLESPOONS ONION POWDER
2 TABLESPOONS GARLIC POWDER
2 TABLESPOONS DRIED OREGANO
1 TABLESPOON GROUND CUMIN
5 BAY LEAVES
6 TABLESPOONS WORCESTERSHIRE SAUCE
1 TABLESPOON FRESHLY GROUND BLACK PEPPER
2¼ POUNDS (1 KG) BEEF CHUCK ROAST
8 CUPS (2 L) VEGETABLE STOCK

ROPA VIEJA

OLIVE OIL, FOR BROWNING
3 SCALLIONS, THINLY SLICED
1 RED BELL PEPPER, SEEDED AND DICED
1 GREEN BELL PEPPER, SEEDED AND DICED
1 (2½-OUNCE/70 G) CAN TOMATO PASTE
½ CUP (100 G) PITTED GREEN OLIVES
1 (1-POUND/450 G) CAN CHOPPED TOMATOES, WITH LIQUID
SALT AND FRESHLY GROUND BLACK PEPPER
SEVERAL SPRIGS PARSLEY, FINELY CHOPPED

MOROS Y CRISTIANOS (PAGE 24), FOR SERVING

To prepare the beef, mix together the beer, onion powder, garlic powder, oregano, cumin, bay leaves, Worcestershire sauce, and pepper in a large bowl, and marinate the beef in this mixture for 30 minutes.

Heat the stock to a simmer in a large pot and add the beef along with the marinade. Simmer the beef in the stock, covered, for at least 3 hours. If you want, you can simmer it for 4 to 5 hours; then it'll be even more tender and easier to shred!

Transfer the beef from the pot to a large bowl. Shred it finely using two forks. It's easy to do and it'll start your mouth watering.

Heat the olive oil in a large pot over medium heat and sauté the scallions, bell peppers, and tomato paste for 3 to 4 minutes. Cut the olives into rings and add the olives and chopped tomatoes to the vegetables, stirring the mixture for several minutes until it's uniformly mixed. Add the shredded beef and season with salt and pepper to taste. Remove the pot from the heat and stir in the chopped parsley.

Serve with *moros y cristianos*—bon appétit!

MOROS Y CRISTIANOS
BLACK BEANS AND RICE

Cuban cuisine almost always includes *congris* or *moros y cristianos* ("Moors and Christians"), a mixture of black beans and rice. This dish—in different versions called by different names—is a popular side dish throughout Latin America.

SERVES 4

1 CUP (200 G) BLACK BEANS, SOAKED FOR AT LEAST 12 HOURS IN LOTS OF WATER
2 BAY LEAVES
5 TABLESPOONS OLIVE OIL
1 SMALL YELLOW ONION, DICED
2 CLOVES GARLIC, MINCED
12 SLICES (50 G) BACON, DICED

½ GREEN BELL PEPPER, SEEDED AND DICED
⅓ CUP (80 ML) WHITE WINE
1 CUP (200 G) RICE
1 TEASPOON GROUND CUMIN
1 TEASPOON DRIED OREGANO
SALT AND FRESHLY GROUND BLACK PEPPER

Rinse and drain the beans and place in a pot along with the bay leaves and lots of fresh water and bring to a boil. Simmer for about 1 hour, or until tender. Drain the beans, reserving the cooking water, and discard the bay leaves.

Heat the olive oil in a skillet over low heat and sauté the onion, garlic, bacon, and bell pepper. This mixture is called a sofrito. Add the white wine to the sofrito, then add 1⅔ cups (400 ml) of the reserved bean-cooking water, along with the beans themselves.

Add the rice, cumin, and oregano to the sofrito-bean mixture. Simmer over low heat until the rice has absorbed the water and is fully cooked, about 30 to 35 minutes. Then simply season it with salt and pepper, and it's ready!

Yojani and Frank, two 23yG crew members who were the same age as us, invited us to stay at Frank's mother's house. His mother, Isa, is an architect and artist who doesn't think much of the Communist regime. Her house is a regular shelter for surfers and skaters from around the world. Frank rides a BMX, Yojani a skateboard. Both are also unbelievably good surfers. In 2008, Frank was even invited by the International Olympic Committee to represent Cuba in the Pan American Surfing Games in Brazil, but was unable to go due to the Communist government's strict travel policies. He still hasn't gotten over it.

Because they're so persecuted, skaters and surfers in Cuba are a close-knit community. They all know and help each other because they all share the same problems. There's no place to buy equipment in Cuba. There isn't a single skate or surf shop in all of Cuba, and there aren't even skate shoes. Some skaters who seemed especially desperate even tried to talk us out of our old, worn-out sneakers. The only way these guys can get new equipment is if somebody actually brings it from another country and leaves it with them.

Such scarcity makes people inventive, and it's impressive to see how creative these guys are when it comes to compensating. Just take an old metal chair leg, some gaffer's tape, a soldering iron, and a tripod head and you've got an instant hand rig for filming skate videos. Frank simply saws the front third off a surfboard, shortens the board by about 8 inches (20 centimeters), and glues it back together. He now has a 6-foot 1-inch shortboard. What's even more amazing is that with this do-it-yourself apparatus he still manages to do aerials off the waves.

If left to ourselves, we probably would never have known that there was surfing in Havana—not if Frank hadn't shown us photos of perfect tubes in the middle of Havana, in the Vedado quarter just off Calle 10.

YOJANI DONATES
HIS WHEELS TO THE
NEXT GENERATION.

From a culinary point of view, Cuba is at first glance a disappointment. Very few products are available to the average person. In most shops the shelves are almost completely empty or are filled with the same few items—rice, beans, potatoes, and cassava roots. Almost everything that's imported is too expensive for the Cuban population to buy. A jar of olives costs around 4 CUCs (or $4), which is the equivalent of 100 Cuban pesos, the parallel currency used by the Cubans. By way of comparison: The average salary paid by the government is around 30 CUCs per month. Cubans buy most of their food with ration cards. Staples such as rice, meat, salt, and sugar are rationed, but there's also a number of small street stands where a piece of greasy flatbread with a little tomato sauce and cheese substitute is sold as a pizza for about 50 cents.

But if you wander the streets a little, you can find fine little bistros that serve local Cuban cuisine at ridiculously low prices. Most of the dishes consist of a piece of pork with the typical Cuban side of *moros y cristianos* (page 24), a mixture of rice and black beans. These often come with deep-fried plantains and a small salad. It's all topped with *aliño criollo*, a homemade sour vinegar sauce with little chunks of chopped onion, garlic, pepper leaves, and small, mild green chile peppers floating in it, served in a battered plastic bottle. On the street this meal comes in a little cardboard box and is then called *cajita*, as in our Cajita de Cerdo that follows.

CAJITA DE CERDO
PORK IN A BOX

Literal translation: pork in a cardboard box. Here's our own version. If you want, you can get some hamburger boxes and serve it in classic street-food fashion.

SERVES 4

2¼ POUNDS (1 KG) PORK SHOULDER OR PORK BELLY
3 TABLESPOONS OLIVE OIL, PLUS MORE FOR FRYING
1 TEASPOON DRIED OREGANO
1 TEASPOON GROUND CUMIN
2 STALKS CELERY, COARSELY CHOPPED
1 CARROT, PEELED AND COARSELY CHOPPED
1 YELLOW ONION, COARSELY CHOPPED
8 TO 10 SPRIGS PARSLEY, CHOPPED
2 SHOTS DARK RUM
SALT AND FRESHLY GROUND BLACK PEPPER
1 BUNCH CILANTRO, MINCED

MOROS Y CRISTIANOS (PAGE 24), FOR SERVING

1 CUP (240 ML) VEGETABLE OIL, PLUS MORE
FOR THE SALAD
1 PLANTAIN, PEELED AND SLICED
1 GREEN BELL PEPPER, SEEDED AND CHOPPED
1 TOMATO, CHOPPED
½ CUCUMBER, CHOPPED

ALIÑO CRIOLLO (PAGE 52), FOR SERVING

Preheat the oven to 425°F (220°C). Rub the meat with the olive oil, oregano, and cumin. Distribute the celery, carrot, onion and parsley in a deep baking pan or a Dutch oven. Pour on the rum, season with salt and pepper, and place the pork on top. Cook the pork in the oven for 1½ hours, basting it every 20 minutes with the meat juices that form.

Remove the pork from the oven and wrap it in aluminum foil. Pour the rest of the baking dish contents through a strainer and reserve the meat juices, but discard the rest.

Add the cilantro to the *moros y cristianos*. Then add the meat juices and stir until the rice and beans form a creamy mixture. Cover with foil to keep warm.

Heat the vegetable oil in a saucepan and deep-fry the plantain slices for about 2 minutes. Then remove them from the pan and drain them on a plate lined with paper towels. Season with salt to taste.

In a large bowl, toss together the bell pepper, tomato, and cucumber to make a salad. Dress the salad with just a little vegetable oil.

Distribute the rice-bean mixture among four plates. Cut the pork into large cubes, season it with salt and pepper, and distribute it over the four mounds of rice and beans. Arrange the plantain slices next to the pork. Top with a shot of *aliño criollo* and enjoy!

HIDDEN MARKETS

After spending a few days scouring the city on foot, we gradually began to discover hidden corners. Havana was constantly surprising us: At a triangular courtyard market behind the Capitol on Dragones Street, we found an 11-year-old, chain-smoking boy who sold spices from a wooden rack. He had peppercorns, bay leaves, turmeric, cinnamon, paprika, cloves, oregano, cumin, soup spice, and nutmeg—an excellent supply of basic spices for our trip. Eventually we even found an amazingly well-stocked market in our own neighborhood (Playa, Calle 42). Although the mangoes, papayas, pineapples, limes, and lettuce were expensive, at least they were available. In addition to all sorts of fruits and vegetables, they even sold bunches of mint, cilantro, and parsley—our favorite herbs. Loaded up with as many ingredients as we could possibly carry, we made our way home to Isa, already composing in our heads the menu for the family's evening meal: spicy chicken quarters with homemade Caribbean rum salsa, mango salad, deep-fried salted plantains, and lime rice.

COSITA BUENA
MANGO CHICKEN LEGS

This isn't really a typical Cuban dish. It has strong Jamaican influences, and contains a pinch of the desperation we felt as we searched for unusual and original recipes. So what—it's delicious!

SERVES 2

CHICKEN
- 4 CLOVES GARLIC
- 1 TEASPOON SWEET PAPRIKA
- 1 TEASPOON CURRY POWDER
- 1/4 CUP (60 ML) OLIVE OIL
- SALT AND FRESHLY GROUND BLACK PEPPER
- 2 CHICKEN LEG QUARTERS

MANGO SALAD
- 2 MANGOES, PEELED AND DICED
- 1 SCALLION, THINLY SLICED
- 1 BUNCH CILANTRO, MINCED
- FRESHLY SQUEEZED JUICE OF 2 LIMES
- 2 TABLESPOONS COCONUT OIL, MELTED
- 1 TEASPOON CHILI POWDER OR 1 RED CHILE

PEPPER, SEEDED AND MINCED
SALT AND FRESHLY GROUND BLACK PEPPER

LIME RICE
- 1 CUP (200 G) RICE
- PINCH OF SALT
- 1 1/4 CUPS (300 ML) WATER
- 2 KAFFIR LIME LEAVES

RUM KETCHUP (PAGE 50), FOR SERVING

Preheat the oven to 390ºC (200ºC).

To make the chicken, peel the garlic, squeeze it through a press, and combine it with the paprika, curry powder, olive oil, salt, and pepper. Rub this marinade into the chicken leg quarters, place them in a casserole dish, and bake them for about 45 minutes. While they're baking, prepare the side dishes.

To make the mango salad, in a large bowl toss together the mango chunks, scallion, and cilantro. Combine the lime juice, coconut oil, chili powder, salt, and pepper to make a dressing. Just before serving, pour the dressing over the mangoes and scallions and toss the salad.

To make the rice, combine the rice, salt, water, and kaffir lime leaves in a pot and bring it to a boil over medium heat. Lower the heat and cook the rice for 20 minutes, or until it has absorbed all the water and is soft. If it's still a little grainy, add a little more water and cook it for another 5 minutes.

Arrange the chicken, mango salad, and lime rice on two plates and serve with the ketchup.

THE ROOF OF HAVANA

During one of our many explorations of Havana, we suddenly found ourselves in front of a fairly tall building in poor condition (the building, not us). The view from that roof had to be fantastic. Shrugging, we walked right in. After a skeptical examination of the rickety elevator, we decided to take the narrow stairs. Four floors later, we were facing the heavy iron door to the roof. There was a little doorbell on the wall, so we pushed it and waited. A large brown eye peered at us through a crack, and then an enormous woman opened the door, giving us a suspicious look and at the same time smiling broadly. She invited us into her realm—the building's flat roof. Actually she, her husband, their 5-year-old daughter and an overexcited black puppy all lived in a tiny garret in just one corner of the roof—we estimated it to be no more than 107 square feet (10 square meters)—containing two beds, a minimalist kitchen, and a sort of bathroom area. It opened our eyes to another world. The obligatory television set showed dancing Latinas flickering in analog quality. Soup was bubbling on the stove, spreading its seductive fragrance over the entire roof. She let us have a taste. The climb was definitely worth it!

SOPA DE LENTEJAS
ROOFTOP LENTIL SOUP

SERVES 4

6 CUPS (1½ L) VEGETABLE STOCK
¾ CUP (200 G) RED LENTILS
2 CUPS (250 G) DICED CARROTS
1¾ CUPS (250 G) DICED CASSAVA ROOT (OR SUBSTITUTE POTATOES)
1¾ CUPS (250 G) DICED YELLOW SUMMER SQUASH
1 RED CHILE PEPPER, SEEDED AND MINCED
4 CLOVES GARLIC, MINCED

5 BAY LEAVES
1 STAR ANISE
1¾ CUPS (420 ML) COCONUT MILK
1 TABLESPOON CURRY POWDER
1 TEASPOON GROUND TURMERIC
1 TEASPOON GROUND CUMIN
1 TEASPOON GROUND CINNAMON
PINCH OF BROWN SUGAR
JUICE OF 2 LIMES
SALT AND FRESHLY GROUND BLACK PEPPER
SEVERAL SPRIGS CILANTRO, MINCED
SEVERAL SPRIGS MINT, MINCED

Heat the vegetable stock in a large pot and add the lentils, carrots, cassava, squash, chile pepper, garlic, bay leaves, star anise, and coconut milk. Stir everything together thoroughly, cover the pot, and simmer over low heat for 20 minutes. Continue to stir occasionally so it won't burn to the bottom of the pot.

Add the curry powder, turmeric, cumin, and cinnamon. Let the soup stand for another 5 minutes. Add the brown sugar and lime juice, and season with salt and pepper to taste. Sprinkle the cilantro and mint over the top, and it's done—dig in!

THEY MAY NOT HAVE MUCH, BUT THERE'S ONE THING THAT NO ONE CAN TAKE AWAY FROM THEM. EVERY EVENING THEY HAVE THE FINEST VIEW OF HAVANA'S MAGICAL SUNSET.

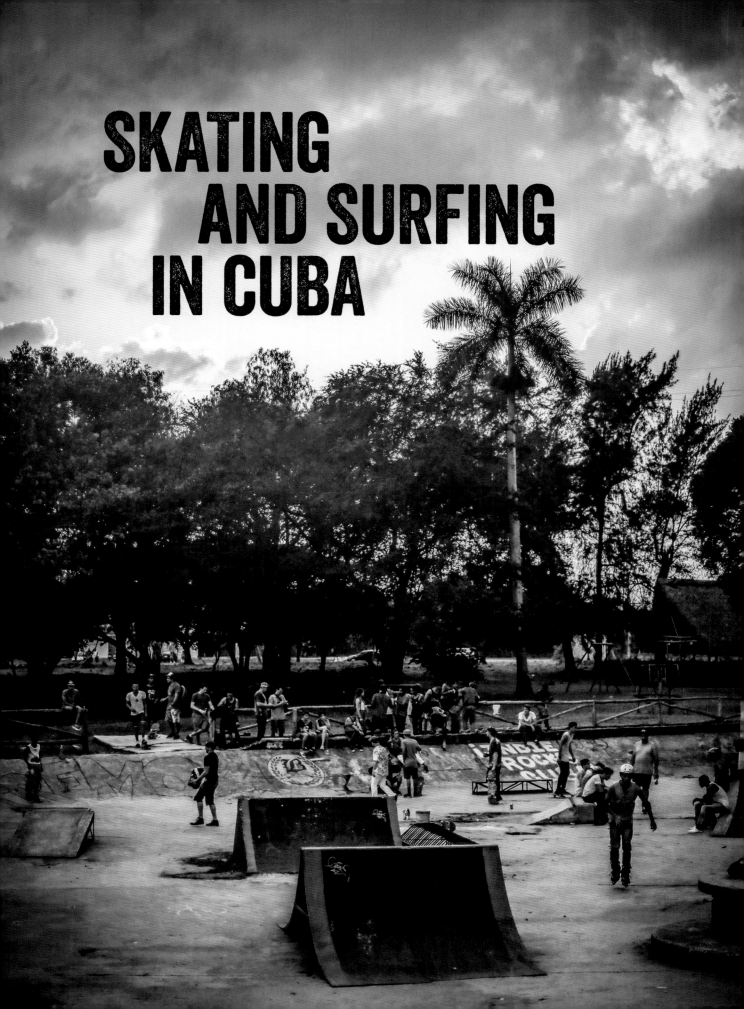

SKATING AND SURFING IN CUBA

Cuba has skaters and lots of surfers, even beyond the 23yG crew. The guys and girls who practice this exotic sport reminded us a little of defiant Gauls forced to stand up against the superior power of the Romans. The police are constantly confiscating their boards, and every once in a while, someone spends a night in jail because they took the twelve steps of a marble Communist monument with a frontside flip instead of walking down on their feet.

The rest of the population also looks on these sports with suspicion. Skaters and surfers are seen as good-for-nothing bums and troublemakers. Once when we were surfing off the Malecon, the police called us back to shore. Stupidly, we'd left Cozy alone on the seawall with all the camera equipment and backpacks, filming, while the rest of us surfed. A policeman was now standing next to him, gesticulating wildly and blowing his whistle. Frank and Yojani paddled 1¼ miles (2 kilometers) to the other shore and escaped—in these sorts of confrontations, the police often end up confiscating their boards and throwing them in jail. Swimming at the Malecon is strictly forbidden!

To lend Cozy support, I reluctantly paddled in and climbed up the slippery seawall. As tourists, our friends explained, they couldn't do much to us because tourists in Cuba are untouchable. First came a long discussion with the uniformed guard. All our efforts to explain were wasted. Swimming is prohibited. Sit down. We sat on the seawall beside a nervous cop under a blazing-hot midday sun for two solid hours. The policeman clutched his radio, every five minutes calling for backup that never came.

Finally at one point, a truck carrying more policemen on its bed stopped in front of us. One of the policemen jumped down and spoke briefly with our surf-police guard, who then climbed onto the truck and disappeared with the rest of them. So now we waited in the heat of a Cuban afternoon with another uniformed clown. He obviously had no idea why he was guarding us, but he did his best. Another hour passed before the long-awaited squad car finally came. Out climbed the chief, who gave the order: Load everything into the car and take 'em down to the station!

By now we were starting to get worried. We had absolutely no desire to get caught up in Cuban police bureaucracy. Obediently, we loaded all the backpacks into the trunk of the squad car, wondering what was in store for us when we finally reached the station. But then came an impossible dilemma: The surfboards wouldn't fit into the squad car. Three policemen stood around the car, frowning and thinking. While they heatedly discussed the situation, we laughed to ourselves. Finally, they came up with an extremely simple and surprising solution: Take everything out again! Go home! Don't do it again! Uh— OK, bye, see you tomorrow.

What was for us just a close shave happens to skaters and surfers in Cuba all the time, but without the protection of being tourists. If we'd been Cuban they would, at the very least, have taken our boards and thrown us in jail. Such experiences are painful, but they also serve to bring the local board-sports community even closer together. Skaters and surfers help each other out. If someone breaks their board, two people share. The older members teach their tricks to the younger, and they repair anything that breaks by pooling their knowledge and improvisational skills. If anyone gets new equipment, they give their old gear away. It's like one big family. Some members of the crew are currently working on opening Cuba's first surf bar and restaurant. They already have the first item for their menu—the Cubano Sandwich, which you'll find on the next page.

FRANK EXECUTING
A SKILLFUL
VIOLATION OF THE
SWIMMING BAN
AT THE MALECON.

CUBAN SANDWICH

We hope you're not religious, because this hefty sandwich is a sin. A genuine Cuban street-food classic. It's not exactly good for you, but it tastes SUPREME. Our suggestion: Follow this sandwich with partial penance in the form of a swim workout.

MAKES 8 SANDWICHES

2¼ POUNDS (1 KG) PORK SHOULDER OR PORK ROAST WITH THE SKIN (OR COLD LEFTOVER PORK ROAST!)
1 MEDIUM WHITE ONION, PEELED
3 BAY LEAVES
1¼ TEASPOONS GROUND CUMIN
PINCH OF SUGAR
SALT AND FRESHLY GROUND BLACK PEPPER
8 LARGE PANINI ROLLS OR OTHER ITALIAN OR FRENCH BREAD ROLLS
MUSTARD
MAYONNAISE (PAGE 51)
1 POUND (500 G) COOKED HAM, SLICED
32 PICKLE SLICES
16 SLICES SWISS CHEESE
4 TABLESPOONS (50 G) BUTTER, MELTED

Place the pork, peeled onion, and bay leaves in a large pot filled with water. Bring the water to a boil, and simmer the pork for 3 hours. Make sure the pork is always completely covered with liquid.

Preheat the oven to 400°F (200°C).

Remove the pork from the water and pat it thoroughly dry. Finely grind the cumin, sugar, and salt and pepper to taste in a mortar and pestle and rub this mixture into the pork shoulder. Place the pork on a baking sheet and bake it for 15 minutes. The prolonged boiling makes the pork as soft as butter on the inside, while rapid baking in the oven gives it a nice crust on the outside. Baking also caramelizes the sugar on the skin, giving the pork a sweet, smoky note. Normally this sandwich calls for pulled pork, which would mean smoking the meat in a smoker for at least 18 hours. Our version is much quicker!

Cut the rolls in half lengthwise. Spread the bottom halves with mustard and the top halves with mayonnaise. Take the pork out of the oven and shred it using two forks. Season it once again with salt and pepper and mix it with a little of the meat juices from the baking sheet.

Distribute the pork on the 8 bottom rolls and cover it with the ham. Top each sandwich with 4 pickle slices and 2 cheese slices, and then replace the roll tops. Spread a little melted butter on top of each sandwich and toast them in a sandwich toaster, panini press or a stovetop griddle or pan for 1 to 2 minutes—and the famous Cuban sandwich is ready to eat.

CUBA SURF GUIDE

We had Yojani and Frank write the surf guide for Cuba, because if anyone knows where to find waves in Cuba, it's those two!

Cuba has waves only in the winter when the huge Atlantic swells pass between the Bahamas upstream. It isn't constant, but when the swells do come, you'll find excellent waves in several spots.

PLAYA SETENTA 23.11175°N -82.44205°E

Our favorite spot in Havana has bathtub-warm Caribbean waves breaking over a reef. Under perfect conditions, you'll have glassy barrels. You'll find the wave in the Playa district where 70th Street ends at the water, directly in front of the Hotel Neptuno-Tritón.

There's a left peak and a right peak. *Comegofios* (a slang term for anyone from the Canary Islands) generally stay to the left and regulars to the right. This spot makes a brutal first impression because the entrance crosses a sharp-edged reef. But with a depth of around 4 feet (1.2 meters), you'll have enough water under you to feel safe.

EL CAYO 23.09891°N -82.45471°E

This spot is in the Playa district on Avenida 3a at the level of Calle 112, just before La Isla del Coco amusement park. One of the island's best waves breaks here, with rides up to 18 seconds long. There are lefts and rights and the water isn't too shallow. Good for beginners!

LA SOCIEDAD 23.09365°N -82.48455°E

Here there are rights and lefts about 131 feet (40 meters) out at the Playa Jaimanitas fishing beach. The right is less dangerous because it's less shallow than the left, but the left has barrel sections.

EL BAJO (MALECON) 23.13839°N -82.40707°E

As the name implies, this spot is at the Malecon—or more specifically, where the Río Almendares empties into the ocean on the east side of the estuary at the level of Calle 10. As is usual near a river mouth, the water is sometimes pretty filthy. But note: Sometimes you get harassed by the police because swimming is officially prohibited at the Malecon. This is Frank Gonzales's favorite spot, but it takes nerves and experience to surf here. Sharp rocks are lurking everywhere and the water is only about as deep as a hot tub. But if you want to surf the best tubes of your life, you'll have to come here—it has the best tubes in all of Cuba.

PLAYA SETENTA

Yojani also has a tip about an awesome spot on the eastern side of the island. Unfortunately, we never had a chance to surf there ourselves:

BOCA DE YUMURI 20.51370°N –74.65098°E

This spot is on the northeast side of Cuba, 15 minutes south of the village of Baracoa. It's a paradise with 656- to 985-foot-wide (200 to 300 meter) tubes at a river mouth above a rocky sea floor. Depending on the swells, it's good both to the right and to the left of the river. Just next door is a tiny indigenous fishing village where the people eat only what they catch or grow themselves. If you go there ask for Roberto, a friendly surfer who likes to show off his home waves and the special sights of this Caribbean paradise.

In short: If you're a surfer and visitor to Cuba, you must surf Setenta and Yumuri, otherwise all you've done is tour another island.

GRAFFITI IN CUBA

Marcos explained to us that the few graffiti artists who live here make their own paints by mixing pigments from printer cartridges with gasoline. Although they can buy bad cans of cheap auto paint and fill them with their own mixture, one can costs the equivalent of about $4.50 (4 euros). Nobody here can afford that many cans, so they have to use brushes for blending their colors. They generally paint dilapidated buildings left over from the Soviets, or they might ask permission from the owner of a wall they particularly like. Most people here won't say no to free wall painting.

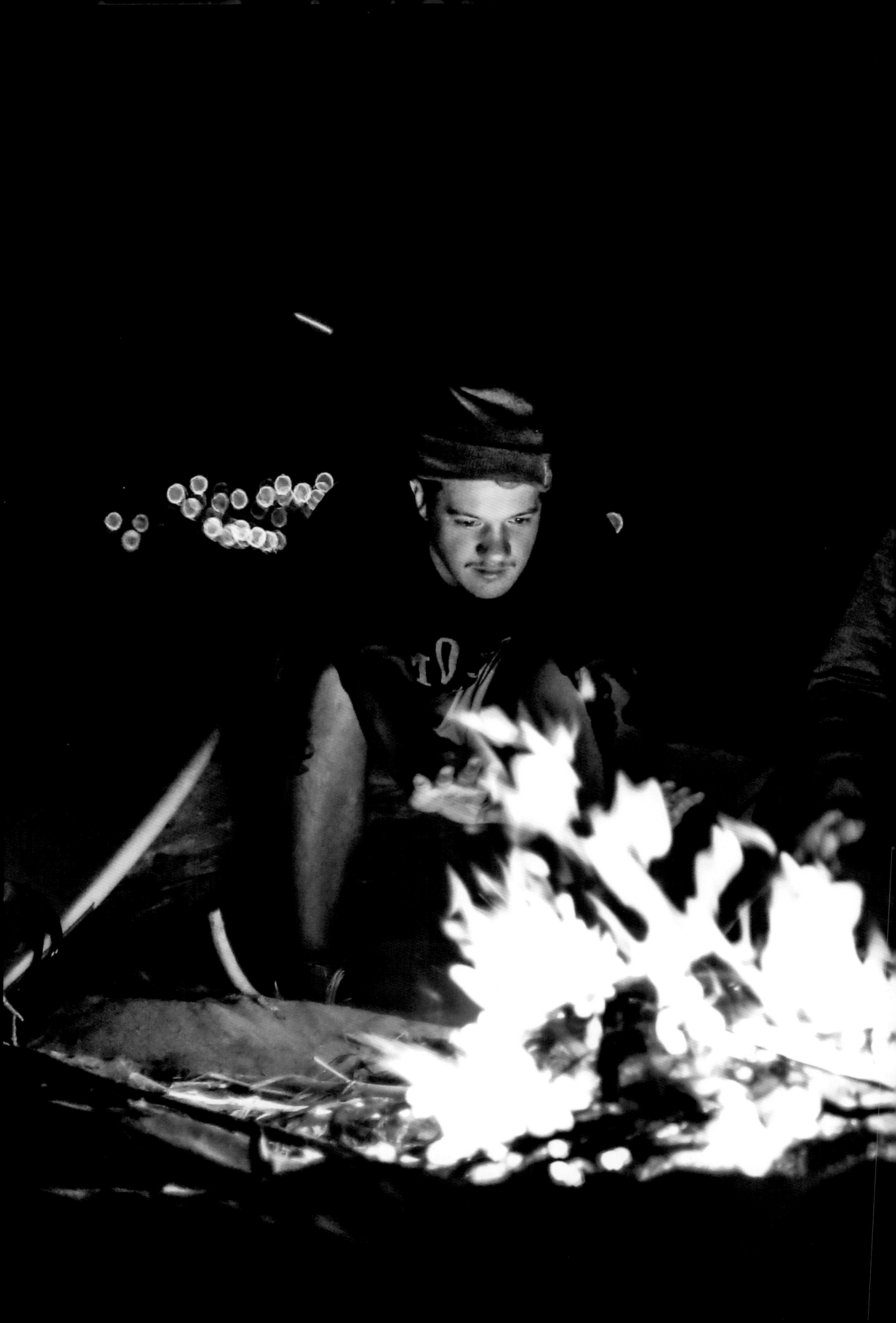

BASIC PROVISIONS

Imagine you're sitting on the beach after a strenuous surf session, you've just roasted a juicy, crusty piece of meat on a stick over a fire, and now you have to eat it without a glob of the world's best barbecue sauce. Oh, the horror!

Or just as bad: You're on a road trip and you wind up in a small fishing village where an old man is selling fresh lobsters out of the trunk of his car, but you don't have any homemade chipotle-lime sauce on you. The very thought brings tears to your eyes.

To avoid such disaster, we generally travel with a couple of canning jars and are constantly preparing a fresh supply of sauces, salsas, and chutneys for the days to come. A splotch of Caribbean Pesto (page 55) turns a toasted roll into a holiday treat, and some homemade Plum, Coconut, and Lemongrass Marmalade (page 54) in the morning consoles you against the fact that the only shop for miles around carries nothing but moldy instant coffee. At night after a bottle of rum, you'll be beside yourself with joy when you can dip cold grilled meat left over from dinner into a sweet-and-spicy yellow bell pepper sauce. Don't miss out on these moments. Be prepared and learn by heart our recipes for basic provisions on the next few pages.

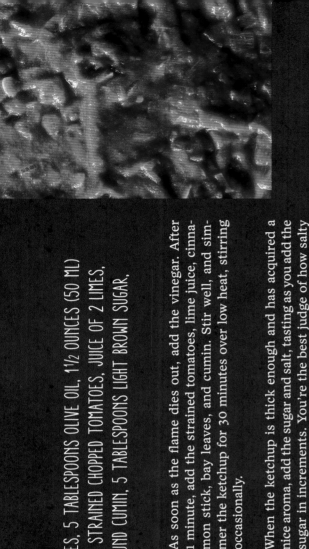

RUM KETCHUP

2 SMALL WHITE ONIONS, 5 CLOVES GARLIC, 2 TOMATOES, 5 TABLESPOONS OLIVE OIL, 1½ OUNCES (50 ML) DARK RUM, ¼ CUP (60 ML) VINEGAR, 1¾ CUPS (400 G) STRAINED CHOPPED TOMATOES, JUICE OF 2 LIMES, ½ CINNAMON STICK, 3 BAY LEAVES, 1 TEASPOON GROUND CUMIN, 5 TABLESPOONS LIGHT BROWN SUGAR, OR AS NEEDED, PINCH OF SALT

Peel and mince the onions and garlic. Remove the seeds from the tomatoes and dice them finely. Heat the olive oil in a saucepan over low heat and cook the onions and garlic until translucent. Then add the chopped tomatoes and cook for another 3 minutes.

Add the rum and carefully light it on fire. A simple trick: light a dry piece of spaghetti—then you won't burn your fingers! Stir the sauce well while the alcohol is burning off so that it all mixes together nicely.

As soon as the flame dies out, add the vinegar. After 1 minute, add the strained tomatoes, lime juice, cinnamon stick, bay leaves, and cumin. Stir well, and simmer the ketchup for 30 minutes over low heat, stirring occasionally.

When the ketchup is thick enough and has acquired a nice aroma, add the sugar and salt, tasting as you add the sugar in increments. You're the best judge of how salty or sweet you want your ketchup to be. That's all there is to it! Pour it into a sterilized bottle and stand it upside-down for 5 minutes. Refrigerated, the ketchup will keep for about 2 weeks.

SALSA VERDE

This sauce is awesome with fish and meat, or even potatoes. It's much healthier than ketchup and the fresh herbs give it a nice, refreshing flavor. When we make it, half the sauce usually ends up going straight from the blender into our mouths.

1 LARGE BUNCH CILANTRO, 1 LARGE BUNCH PARSLEY, LEAVES ONLY, 1 LARGE BUNCH MINT, LEAVES ONLY, 1 CUP (240 ML) OLIVE OIL, 1 HEAPING TEASPOON MUSTARD, 2 TABLESPOONS CAPERS (OPTIONAL), 2 ANCHOVY FILLETS (OPTIONAL), JUICE OF 1 LEMON, SALT (OPTIONAL)

Place the cilantro, parsley, and mint in a blender along with ½ cup of the olive oil. Add the mustard, capers, anchovy fillets, and lemon juice. If you use capers and anchovies the sauce will automatically be salty enough. If you leave out these ingredients you'll need to add some salt.

Start up the blender and blend into a thick paste. You'll have to adjust the amount of oil depending on the size of your herb bunches. Gradually add more oil until you have a runny herb mixture, occasionally switching on the blender for short bursts. Pour the salsa into a clean jar. Refrigerated, the salsa will keep for about 1 week.

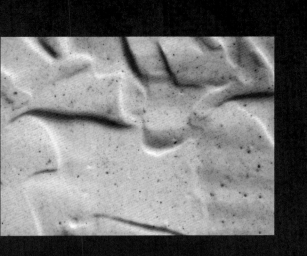

CHIPOTLE-LIME SAUCE

Few things in this world taste better dipped in a hot-and-sour mayonnaise than breaded and baked or deep-fried shrimp. The combination will blow you away. This dip always turns out perfectly if you make it with store-bought mayonnaise, but if you're especially industrious, you can of course make your own mayo.

FOR THOSE WHO PREFER THE SIMPLE SURF-TRIP VERSION WITH STORE-BOUGHT MAYO:

4 TABLESPOONS MAYONNAISE

JUICE OF 1 LIME

1 TABLESPOON RED WINE VINEGAR

1 TEASPOON MUSTARD

3 DASHES TABASCO OR OTHER HOT SAUCE

1 HEAPING TEASPOON CAYENNE PEPPER

1 TEASPOON TURBINADO SUGAR

FRESHLY GROUND BLACK PEPPER

MAKES 5 OUNCES (ABOUT 150 G)

Just mix everything together thoroughly and it's done! Transfer the sauce to a clean jar. Refrigerated, the sauce will keep for about 10 days.

FOR THOSE WHO LIKE TO DO IT THEMSELVES: HERE'S OUR BASIC MAYO RECIPE!

2 LARGE EGG YOLKS, PREFERABLY ORGANIC

PINCH OF SALT

PINCH OF SUGAR

1/3 CUP (80 ML) PEANUT OIL

3/4–1 CUP (180–240 ML) SUNFLOWER OIL

MAKES 11 OUNCES (ABOUT 330 G)

Place the egg yolks in a large bowl. Add the salt and sugar and beat the yolks with a wire whisk to thicken them slightly. Then add a few drops of peanut oil—no more than 1/2 teaspoon—and whisk vigorously and thoroughly until the oil and egg yolks become a homogenous mixture. Add a few more drops of oil. Be very careful not to add too many drops at a time or your mayo won't thicken properly. Mayo is finicky—sometimes it doesn't matter what you do, you just can't keep it from separating! After about 3 teaspoons of oil, the mayo should slowly start to thicken. Then you can add the oil in a thin stream. But never stop whisking!

When you've used up all the peanut oil, continue with the sunflower oil. You may not use all the sunflower oil. If your mayo thickens sooner, leave out the remainder.

Refrigerated in an airtight container, the mayonnaise will keep for 8 to 10 days, but it's safer to use it up immediately.

ALIÑO CRIOLLO
CREOLE SALSA

MAKES 14 OUNCES
(ABOUT 400 G)

This hot-and-sour sauce is part of Cuban cuisine. It goes especially well with pork but also makes a nice dressing for a side salad. In Cuba, this extraordinary sauce is usually found in battered plastic bottles on the tables of streetside restaurants. It keeps for a long time and is easy to make.

2 SMALL GREEN CHILE PEPPERS, SEVERAL CILANTRO STEMS, 2 CLOVES GARLIC, 1 CUP (240 ML) APPLE CIDER VINEGAR, 5 TABLESPOONS EXTRA-VIRGIN OLIVE OIL, JUICE OF 2 LIMES, 2 BAY LEAVES, 1 STAR ANISE, 1 TEASPOON SALT, ½ TEASPOON GROUND CUMIN

Remove the seeds from the chile peppers and cut the peppers into thin rings. Chop the cilantro. Peel and crush the garlic. Place all of the ingredients in a clean bottle and shake well. Refrigerated, the sauce will keep for several weeks. The longer it stands, the spicier and hotter it becomes.

NICA SAUCE
NICARAGUAN SALSA

This sauce is at its best when you sear chicken and add a generous shot to the pan. It's also excellent with the Grilled Vegetable Teriyaki Salad on page 124. Or you can use it as a marinade for grilled meat or to brown chicken—this sauce does it all!

MAKES 17 OUNCES
(ABOUT 500 ML)

1 CLOVE GARLIC
2¼ INCHES (6 CM) FRESH GINGER
1 TEASPOON COCONUT OIL
⅓ CUP (80 ML) DARK RUM
⅓ CUP (80 ML) SOY SAUCE
4 TABLESPOONS HONEY
JUICE OF 1 LIME
1 TABLESPOON TURBINADO SUGAR
1 TEASPOON CAYENNE PEPPER
½ TEASPOON GROUND CINNAMON

Peel the garlic and ginger and grate both finely. Melt the coconut oil in a small saucepan over low heat and soften the garlic and ginger in the oil for about 3 minutes. At the very end, turn the heat up to high and carefully add the rum.

After the rum has cooked off (takes about 3 to 6 minutes) add the soy sauce, honey, lime juice, sugar, cayenne, and cinnamon to the saucepan, along with 3½ tablespoons (50 ml) water. Decrease the heat and simmer the sauce for another 5 minutes. Pour the sauce into a glass bottle and stand it upside down for 5 minutes. Refrigerated, the sauce will keep for about 2 weeks.

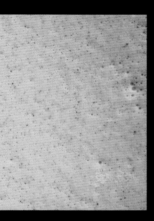

CILANTRO SALSA

1 CUP (240 ML) SOY SAUCE
1/3 CUP (80 ML) OLIVE OIL
1/2 CUP (120 ML) SUNFLOWER OIL
1 1/2 INCHES (4 CM) FRESH
GINGER, FINELY GRATED
1 BUNCH CILANTRO, CHOPPED

1 TABLESPOON SUGAR
JUICE OF 2 LIMES, OR
AS NEEDED
SALT (OPTIONAL)

Pour the soy sauce into a blender and switch it on to the lowest setting. With the blender running, gradually add the olive oil and then the sunflower oil in a thin stream until the oils are emulsified.

With the blender still running, add the ginger, cilantro, and sugar. Then add the lime juice and salt at the very end—preferably not all at once. You might like your salsa less sour than we do. Pour the salsa into a clean jar. Refrigerated, it will keep for about 1 week.

MANGO CHUTNEY

2 MANGOES (NOT TOO RIPE OR SOFT), 1 SMALL RED ONION, 2 CLOVES GARLIC, 1 RED CHILE PEPPER, 2 TABLESPOONS OLIVE OIL, 1 TEASPOON HONEY, 1/2 CUP (1/8 L) WHITE WINE VINEGAR, JUICE OF 2 LIMES, OR AS NEEDED, 1 TEASPOON GROUND CINNAMON, OR AS NEEDED, 1/2 TEASPOON GROUND CUMIN, OR AS NEEDED, 2 KAFFIR LIME LEAVES

Peel and dice the mangoes. Peel the onion and cut it into eighths. Peel the garlic and squeeze it through a press. Remove the seeds from the chile pepper and chop the pepper finely.

In a small saucepan, heat the olive oil over medium heat and cook the onions until they're soft, translucent, and slightly brown and sizzled around the edges, about 10 minutes. Add the diced mango, garlic, chile pepper, honey, and vinegar. Lower the heat and simmer this mixture for about 15 minutes, stirring regularly to keep it from sticking to the pan.

Season the chutney to taste with the lime juice, cumin, and cinnamon, and add the kaffir lime leaves. While it's still hot, transfer the chutney to a glass jar and stand the jar upside down for 5 minutes.

Let the chutney cool, and refrigerate it for at least a few hours before serving. Then you'll see how its structure has changed. The chutney develops a fantastic sweet-and-sour flavor. In a sterilized jar, this will keep for at least 4 months. If you didn't sterilize the jar, it will keep for about 2 weeks.

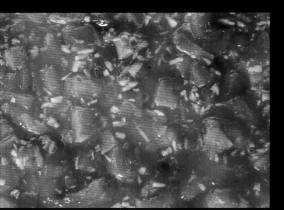

PLUM, COCONUT, AND LEMONGRASS MARMALADE

1 CARDAMOM POD
1 WHOLE CLOVE
2 CUPS (300 G) DICED PLUMS
2 LEMONGRASS STEMS, TENDER INTERIOR ONLY
2 TABLESPOONS GRATED FRESH COCONUT
JUICE OF 1 ORANGE
4¾ TABLESPOONS (70 G) PECTIN
1 TABLESPOON STEVIA POWDER (35 G)

MAKES 16 OUNCES (ABOUT 450 G)

Remove the seeds from the cardamom pod and grind the cardamom seeds and clove in a mortar and pestle. Place all of the ingredients in a pot, stir well, and bring to a boil.

Simmer the marmalade for 10 minutes. While it's still hot, transfer the marmalade to a glass jar and stand the jar upside down for 5 minutes. If you sterilized the jar, the marmalade will keep for several months or even a year or so. If you didn't sterilize the jar, it will keep for 2 weeks.

PERSIMMON, GINGER, GRAPEFRUIT, AND CHILE MARMALADE

1 ALLSPICE BERRY
½ POUND (300 G) PERSIMMON, DICED
2 INCHES (5 CM) FRESH GINGER, GRATED
½ RED CHILE PEPPER, SEEDED AND MINCED
2 INCHES GRATED PEEL FROM LIME
JUICE OF 1 LIME
JUICE OF ½ GRAPEFRUIT
3½ OUNCES (100 G) GELLING SUGAR WITH STEVIA

MAKES 16 OUNCES (ABOUT 450 G)

Grind the allspice berry finely in a mortar and pestle. Place all the ingredients in a pot, stir well, and bring to a boil. Simmer the marmalade for 10 minutes. While it's still hot, transfer the marmalade to a sterilized canning jar and stand the jar upside-down for 5 minutes. If everything's well sterilized, the marmalade keeps for months or even years.

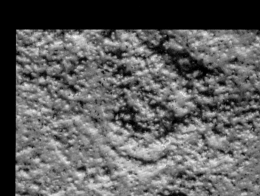

POMELO-AVOCADO DIP

½ POMELO, PEELED AND SECTIONED
1 GREEN BELL PEPPER, SEEDED AND CHOPPED
1 AVOCADO, PITTED AND PEELED
1 SCALLION, GREEN PART ONLY
1 CUP FRESH CILANTRO LEAVES
1 CUP FRESH PARSLEY LEAVES
6 TABLESPOONS (89 ML) OLIVE OIL
1 TEASPOON SALT
FRESHLY GROUND BLACK PEPPER

MAKES 21 OUNCES (ABOUT 600 G)

Combine all of the ingredients in a blender on medium speed and—it's ready to eat! Refrigerated in an airtight container, the dip will keep for up to 1 week.

CARIBBEAN PESTO

½ CUP (80 G) MIXED NUTS (SUCH AS WALNUTS, CASHEWS, BRAZIL NUTS, ALMONDS, PEANUTS)
2¾ OUNCES (80 G) SOFT AGED GOAT CHEESE
1 BUNCH CILANTRO
25 FRESH BASIL LEAVES
3 TABLESPOONS GRATED FRESH COCONUT
1 GREEN CHILE PEPPER
¾ CUP (180 ML) COCONUT MILK
JUICE OF 1 LIME

MAKES 21 OUNCES (ABOUT 600 G)

Combine all of the ingredients (yes, the whole chile with the seeds!) in a blender on medium speed—and you're done! Refrigerated in an airtight container, this will keep for up to 1 week.

BREAKFAST GRANOLA

We never take a surf trip without this perfect—nonperishable, healthy, delicious—instant breakfast. Combined with a little yogurt or milk and fresh fruit, it's a perfect start to any day. You can vary the nuts, seeds, and dried fruits depending on what's available locally. This recipe comes from our friend Claudio, a surfing chef from Chile.

MAKES ABOUT 4 CUPS (600 G)

1¼ CUPS (200 G) OLD-FASHIONED OATS

¾ CUP (100 G) TRAIL MIX (REMOVE AND SET ASIDE THE RAISINS, AS THEY SHOULDN'T BE BAKED)

⅓ CUP (50 G) FLAXSEEDS

¼ CUP (30 G) WHITE SESAME SEEDS

2½ TABLESPOONS (50 G) HONEY

¼ CUP (50 G) LIGHT BROWN SUGAR

¾ TEASPOON GROUND CINNAMON

1 WHOLE CLOVE

PINCH OF FLEUR DE SEL

3 DRIED FIGS, MINCED

MILK OR YOGURT, AND FRUITS OF YOUR CHOICE, FOR SERVING

Preheat the oven to 300°F (150°C). In a large baking dish, mix together the oats, trail mix, flaxseeds, sesame seeds, honey, brown sugar, cinnamon, clove, and salt. Bake for 20 minutes, stirring occasionally so that the mixture toasts evenly. Your granola should come out lightly browned and acquire a heavenly fragrance.

Stir in the dried figs and reserved raisins. Serve the granola with a little milk or yogurt and fresh fruit.

Sealed in a zipper-top freezer bag, granola easily keeps for several weeks, but you'll probably eat it all in a couple of days.

After almost two months in Havana, it was time to move on. We were able to experience Havana from a perspective that would normally be totally inaccessible, far from the "Buena Vista Social Club" style of romanticism that we're programmed to think of as authentic Cuban life. Together with our friends, we visited hidden black markets, we painted graffiti on dilapidated Russian military buildings using homemade gasoline-based paint, we drank home-distilled courtyard rum, and we threw wild house parties. We hated to go. As a parting gift, the 23yG tattoo artist Tere did us the special honor of tattooing us with the 23yG logo. We'll be back!

GUADALAJARA

Sayulita / San Pancho

LA Lancha

Burros

Pascuales

LA Ticla

Rio Nexpa

Welcome to the land of superhot salsas and massive waves. The sun always shines, the mangoes are sweet, and everything is cheap. A paradise—if it weren't for those nasty little problems with drug cartels and corrupt cops.

Our first destination was Guadalajara, Mexico's second largest city. Almost all the walls were painted bright colors, and there were all sorts of busy markets and street food on every corner. Our German friend Mara, who'd been living in Guadalajara for several years, offered to let us stay in her parents' fully furnished, uninhabited vacation home. It was insane—we'd only just arrived and already had our own place to crash for free. Such outrageously good luck!

Gulf
of
MeXiCo

CIUDAD DE
MÉXICO

ACAPULCO

Puerto
Escondido

We tasted our first real tacos at a street-food stand—and oh my god, we had no idea! What passes for "Mexican food" in other countries has absolutely nothing to do with what we found there. A good taco should appeal to your sense of taste in every conceivable way. The corn tortillas are small, paper-thin, and slightly sweet. All the different types of meat are juicy on the inside, crusty on the outside, and spicy. The sauces harmonize perfectly, from mild to hot, with limes, cilantro, and chopped onions to round everything out. The overall combination is phenomenal.

Even though we ate tacos every day, we never got tired of them. They came filled with everything imaginable: calf tongue, cow eyes, chorizo, mushrooms, deep-fried tripe, fish, shrimp, cactus, lips, pork knuckles that had been simmered for hours, and a thousand other fillings. In other words: Try the tacos!

TORTILLAS, SALSAS & GARNISHES

②

③

④

⑤

⑥

⑦

TORTILLAS

The tortilla is the foundation of a good taco. Under NO circumstances should you use commercial tortillas bought from a supermarket. Anyone who does so is legally bound to burn this book immediately (read the small print at the very back).

Seriously, though, the bulky, oversized, cardboard rags that are normally called tortillas won't work for genuine tacos. It's really not hard to make them yourself; you'll be surprised at how little time it takes. And once you've tried the original, you'll never be satisfied with store-bought again. Guaranteed.

It's a good idea to buy yourself a tortilla press—you can get a basic one for $15 to $20 online. Otherwise, we'll explain below how you can make tortillas using two cutting boards.

EACH MAKES 16 TORTILLAS ABOUT 4½ INCHES (12 CM) IN DIAMETER

① CORN TORTILLAS

2¼ CUPS (300 G) HARINA DE MAIZ
(FINE NIXTAMALIZED CORNMEAL;
REGULAR CORNMEAL WON'T WORK)
½ TEASPOON SALT
¾ CUP (180 ML) LUKEWARM WATER,
105°F (40°C)
VEGETABLE OIL, FOR FRYING)

Combine the cornmeal and salt in a bowl and add the lukewarm water. Stir, and then knead the dough thoroughly for 2 minutes.

Take two cutting boards and cover one of them with a 9¾-inch square (25 cm) sheet of plastic wrap. Shape a piece of dough into a 1½-inch (4 cm) ball and place it on top of the plastic wrap.

Cover the dough with a second sheet of plastic wrap. Press the two boards firmly together to flatten the dough into a disk no more than 1/16 inch (2 mm) thick. Remove the top board and carefully peel off the plastic wrap. If you find that the flattened tortilla is fraying around the edges, add a little more water to the dough.

Preheat a nonstick skillet over medium heat. Add a little oil, slide the paper-thin tortilla into the pan, and fry it for about 50 seconds on each side—it should be lightly browned but not too dry or hard.

Line a shallow bowl or a small basket with a kitchen towel. As you cook each tortilla, stack them in the center, and cover them with another kitchen towel. Let the tortillas stand for another 2 minutes before serving so that the dough can rest and become nice and soft.

The tortillas will keep for 1 to 2 days wrapped in plastic at room temperature. Heat again before serving, just to warm them.

② FLOUR TORTILLAS

2½ CUPS (340 G) WHOLE WHEAT FLOUR
1 TEASPOON BAKING POWDER
1 TEASPOON SALT
1 TABLESPOON UNSALTED BUTTER, SOFTENED
¾ CUP (180 ML) LUKEWARM WATER, 105°F (40°C)
VEGETABLE OIL, FOR FRYING

Mix together the flour, baking powder, and salt in a bowl. Knead in the butter until crumbs form. Add the lukewarm water and continue kneading for about 5 to 8 minutes, until you have a firm dough.

Shape the dough into a cylinder and cut it into 16 pieces. Flatten each piece into a thin disk, either in a tortilla press or using the method described on page 66. Fry the tortillas with a little oil in a nonstick skillet over medium heat for 1 to 2 minutes per side. Let them stand for a few minutes before serving. The tortillas will keep for 1 to 2 days wrapped in plastic at room temperature. Heat again before serving, just to warm.

③ SEPIA TORTILLAS (BLACK BEAUTIES)

1 (14-OUNCE) PACKAGE SQUID INK POWDER (FROM A FISH MARKET OR GOURMET SHOP)
2¼ CUPS (300 G) HARINA DE MAIZ (FINE NIXTAMALIZED CORNMEAL)
½ TEASPOON SALT
VEGETABLE OIL, FOR FRYING

Combine the squid ink with ¾ cup (180 ml) water in a bowl. Add the cornmeal and salt and stir, then knead the dough thoroughly for 2 minutes.

Take two cutting boards and cover one of them with a 9¾-inch square (25 cm) sheet of plastic wrap. Shape a piece of dough into a 1½-inch (4 cm) ball and place it on top of the plastic wrap.

Cover the dough with a second sheet of plastic wrap. Press the two boards firmly together to flatten the dough into a disk no more than ¹⁄₁₆ inch (2 mm) thick. Remove the top board and carefully peel off the plastic wrap. If you find that the flattened tortilla is fraying around the edges, add a little more water to the dough.

Preheat a nonstick skillet over medium heat. Add a little oil, slide the paper-thin tortilla into the pan, and fry it for about 50 seconds on each side—it should be lightly browned but not too dry or hard.

Line a shallow bowl or a small basket with a kitchen towel. As you cook each tortilla, stack them in the center, and cover them with another kitchen towel. Let the tortillas stand for another 2 minutes before serving so that the dough can rest and become nice and soft.

The tortillas will keep for 1 to 2 days wrapped in plastic at room temperature. Heat again before serving, just to warm them.

SALSAS AND GARNISHES

Mexican taco stands generally offer at least three different salsas, and often more than that, to add the finishing touch to your tacos. Some of these salsas are always present: a mild, runny avocado salsa; a chopped tomato salsa with onions, garlic, and cilantro; a hot green tomatillo salsa. Besides these salsas, tacos are always accompanied by chopped onions, cilantro, and limes. The one exception is the fish taco, which tastes best with a hot and spicy Chipotle-Lime Sauce (page 51). In Germany, we can buy canned, pickled tomatillos or grow them ourselves from seeds. The leftover salsas and sauces will keep in the refrigerator for up to 2 weeks; or look in the index (page 315) for other recipes to use them with.

④ SALSA CRUDA
BASIC SALSA

MAKES ABOUT 2¾ CUPS (700 G)

6 TOMATOES, CHOPPED
1 CLOVE GARLIC, MINCED
2 SMALL CHILE PEPPERS, SEEDED AND MINCED
1 BUNCH CILANTRO, FINELY CHOPPED
JUICE OF 1 LIME
SALT

Combine the tomatoes, garlic, chile peppers, and cilantro in a bowl. Season with the lime juice and salt to taste and mix thoroughly.

⑤ TACO SALSA VERDE

MAKES ABOUT 2 CUPS (500 G)

½ SMALL YELLOW ONION, QUARTERED
3 JALAPEÑO CHILE PEPPERS, SEEDED
1 (16-OUNCE/450 G) CAN TOMATILLOS
3 TABLESPOONS FRESH CILANTRO LEAVES
SALT AND FRESHLY GROUND BLACK PEPPER

Purée the onion, jalapeño, tomatillos, and cilantro leaves in a blender. Season with salt and pepper to taste—and it's ready to go!

⑥ SALSA AGUACATE
AVOCADO SALSA
MAKES ABOUT 1⅓ CUPS (300 G)

1 AVOCADO, PITTED AND PEELED
½ CLOVE GARLIC
JUICE OF ½ LIME
SALT

Purée the avocado, garlic, lime juice, and 1 cup (240 ml) water in a blender until you have a creamy salsa. At the very end, season with a little salt to taste.

⑦ CHILI OIL

Another very common taco ingredient is spicy chili oil, which mainly consists of dried, smoked chile peppers. It's always great with fried meat and fish. You might as well make a whole bottle, because this stuff keeps forever.

MAKES ABOUT 1¼ CUPS (300 ML)

2 DRIED RED CHILE DE ÁRBOL PEPPERS, CRUSHED
2 SUN-DRIED TOMATOES, CHOPPED
5 TEASPOONS RED PEPPER FLAKES
2 DRIED KAFFIR LIME LEAVES
1 BAY LEAF
1 STAR ANISE
2 ALLSPICE BERRIES
3 TEASPOONS SMOKED PAPRIKA
PINCH OF SALT
2 CLOVES GARLIC
1¼ CUPS (300 ML) OLIVE OIL

Grind the crushed dried red peppers, sun-dried tomatoes, red pepper flakes, kaffir lime leaves, bay leaf, star anise, allspice berries, smoked paprika, and salt to a coarse powder in a mortar and pestle.

Using a funnel, pour your chili powder into a clean, resealable bottle. Peel and crush the garlic and add it to the bottle. Pour in the oil, shake well, and let the aromatic oil stand overnight. The longer it stands, the stronger it'll be and the better it will taste!

TACOS DE HÍGADO
LIVER TACOS

SERVES 3

FILLING

- 1¼ POUNDS (500 G) PORK OR BEEF LIVER
- 1 SMALL RED ONION
- 2 TABLESPOONS VEGETABLE OIL
- ⅓ CUP APPLE CIDER VINEGAR
- 1 CLOVE GARLIC, MINCED
- 1 TEASPOON CAYENNE PEPPER
- ½ TEASPOON GROUND CUMIN
- SALT AND FRESHLY GROUND BLACK PEPPER
- HANDFUL OF CILANTRO LEAVES, MINCED
- JUICE OF 1 LIME

BASE AND TOPPINGS

- 8 TORTILLAS (PAGE 66)
- SALSA CRUDA (PAGE 68)
- SALSA AGUACATE (PAGE 69)
- CHILI OIL (PAGE 69)
- TACO SALSA VERDE (PAGE 68)

To prepare the filling, cut the liver into ⅓ by ¾-inch (1 by 2 cm) pieces. Peel and halve the onion, then cut it into crescents ¼ inch (½ cm) thick.

Heat the oil in a skillet and sauté the onion crescents over medium heat for 7 to 10 minutes, until golden brown. Add the liver and increase the heat to the highest setting. Fry the liver pieces for about 5 minutes.

Add the vinegar to the pan, then add the garlic, cayenne, and cumin. The filling is done when the vinegar has evaporated. (This should take 5 to 7 minutes.) Season the liver with salt and pepper and divide it among the tortillas. Top each with chopped cilantro, a little lime juice, and whatever salsas you prefer—and dig in!

FISH TACOS

**Fish tacos are our absolute favorite.
In Mexico, they usually came with a fantastic
chipotle sauce and lettuce strips.**

SERVES 3

FILLING

1 TABLESPOON COCONUT OIL
1¼ POUNDS (500 G) FISH FILLETS, SUCH AS
TUNA, MAHI-MAHI, OR BONITO
SALT AND FRESHLY GROUND BLACK PEPPER
1 HEART ROMAINE LETTUCE, CUT INTO STRIPS
1 LIME, SLICED INTO 8 WEDGES
1 BUNCH CILANTRO, CHOPPED

BASE AND TOPPINGS

8 TORTILLAS (PAGE 66)
CHIPOTLE—LIME SAUCE (PAGE 51)
SALSA AGUACATE (PAGE 69)

Heat the coconut oil in a nonstick pan and brown
the fish over high heat for 2 to 4 minutes per
side. The fish is perfectly done when it's crisp and
golden-brown in places. Season it with salt and
pepper and cut it into manageable-size pieces.

Place several strips of lettuce on each tortilla, lay
the fish on top, and squeeze a lime wedge over the
fish. Add a little of both sauces and sprinkle on
chopped cilantro. Welcome to paradise.

TACOS DE LENGUA
BEEF TONGUE TACOS

SERVES 3

Lengua means "tongue"—in this case, beef tongue. The tongue is simmered slowly until tender, then seared until crisp, and finally chopped. This is how it's served in markets all over Mexico, and for good reason. We recommend Salsa Cruda (page 68), Salsa Aguacate (page 69), Taco Salsa Verde (page 68), Chili Oil (page 69), chopped cilantro, and lime juice, as well as canned, drained white beans that have been heated.

BASE AND TOPPINGS
8 TORTILLAS (PAGE 66)
SALSAS AND GARNISHES (OPTIONAL; SEE HEADNOTE)

FILLING
1 POUND (500 G) BEEF OR VEAL TONGUE, READY TO USE
1 CARROT, PEELED AND COARSELY CHOPPED
2 STALKS CELERY, COARSELY CHOPPED
1 MEDIUM YELLOW ONION, COARSELY CHOPPED
8 TO 10 SPRIGS PARSLEY, CHOPPED
2 BAY LEAVES
5 WHOLE BLACK PEPPERCORNS
3 TABLESPOONS VEGETABLE OIL
SALT

Bring a large pot of salted water to a boil. Add the tongue, carrot, celery, onion, parsley, bay leaves, and peppercorns to the boiling water. Adjust the temperature so that the ingredients simmer gently but don't bubble out of control like a runaway nuclear reactor. Simmer the tongue for 1½ hours, then remove the pot from the heat and leave the tongue in the water for an additional 30 minutes.

Remove the tongue from the water using a slotted spoon, and pat it dry with paper towels. Cut it into cubes of about ⅓ inch (1 cm). Heat the oil in a large skillet over high heat and fry the tongue for 1 minute. Season with salt.

Arrange the tongue on the prepared tortillas and garnish it with salsas, and other garnishes of your choice. Done.

TACOS DE CHORIZO
SAUSAGE TACOS

SERVES 3

FILLING

4 MEXICAN-STYLE CHORIZO SAUSAGES WITH THE MEAT SQUEEZED OUT OF THE SKINS

OR

2 CLOVES GARLIC
2 DRIED CHILE PEPPERS
1 ALLSPICE BERRY
1 TEASPOON GROUND CUMIN
5 WHOLE BLACK PEPPERCORNS
1 BAY LEAF
1 TEASPOON SMOKED PAPRIKA
SEA SALT
1¼ POUNDS (500 G) GROUND PORK
VEGETABLE OIL, FOR FRYING

BASE AND TOPPINGS

8 TORTILLAS (PAGE 66)
VARIOUS SALSAS (PAGES 50–53 AND 68–69)

Spicy chorizo sausages are the perfect taco filling! You just need to find some good Mexican-style raw chorizo, squeeze the sausage out of the skin, break it up into smaller pieces, and sear it. Since the meat's already spiced, it's foolproof. The only thing that might go wrong is if you can't find good raw chorizo. But you won't have to resort to a frozen pizza, because we have the solution to all your chorizo problems: homemade ground sausage.

If making homemade sausage, peel and chop the garlic into a paste. Grind the chile peppers, allspice berry, cumin, and peppercorns finely in a mortar and pestle. Finely crumble the bay leaf.

Combine the spices from the mortar with the bay leaf, paprika, garlic, and salt, mix well, and add to the ground pork. Heat the oil in a skillet over medium heat and cook the pork until crispy, breaking it up as you cook. If you were able to buy whole chorizo sausages, cook it in the same way.

Distribute the sausage among the prepared tortillas, top with various salsas, and scarf 'em down!

MUSHROOM TACOS

Yes, you can even make fantastic vegan tacos. While surfing at Sayulita, we discovered this awesome alternative using mushrooms instead of meat.

SERVES 3

FILLING
VEGETABLE OIL, FOR FRYING
1 SMALL YELLOW ONION, MINCED
1 CLOVE GARLIC, MINCED
1 KING OYSTER MUSHROOM, COARSELY CHOPPED
3 LARGE BROWN MUSHROOMS, COARSELY CHOPPED
2 SHIITAKE MUSHROOMS, COARSELY CHOPPED
SALT AND FRESHLY GROUND BLACK PEPPER
JUICE OF 1 LIME
1 BUNCH CILANTRO, MINCED

To make the filling, heat the oil in a skillet over medium heat and sauté the onion for 10 to 15 minutes, until translucent. Add the garlic and swirl around the contents of the pan briefly. Add the mushrooms and cook for 10 to 12 minutes. Season the mushroom mixture with salt and pepper and distribute it evenly among the tortillas. Top with a dash of lime juice and cilantro, and the other toppings of your choice, and you'll warm the vegan heart.

BASE AND TOPPINGS
8 TORTILLAS (PAGE 66)
CHILI OIL (PAGE 69)
SALSA CRUDA (PAGE 68)
SALSA AGUACATE (PAGE 69)

On our way to the ocean, we were constantly passing carnitas shacks. *Carnitas*, meaning "little meats," are another essential taco ingredient. In this case, pork is cooked for several hours in lard and spices until it's tender and juicy and practically falling apart. In Mexico, you often see tin vats filled with oil and meat simmering over dying embers by the side of the road. Of course, carnitas aren't exactly good for you...but sometimes you have to sin a little! Forget pork roast and dumplings: Here come the *tacos de carnitas*!

TACOS DE CARNITAS
PULLED-PORK TACOS

SERVES 4

FILLING

18 SLICES (500 G) BACON
2 1/3 CUPS (500 G) LARD
1 1/4 CUPS (300 ML) SUNFLOWER OIL
1 TABLESPOON WHOLE BLACK PEPPERCORNS
3 BAY LEAVES
2 TABLESPOONS SMOKED PAPRIKA
1 DRIED BELL PEPPER
3 DRIED CHILE PEPPERS
1 TABLESPOON DRIED MARJORAM
1 TABLESPOON GROUND CUMIN
1 TABLESPOON DRIED OREGANO
2 3/4 POUNDS (1.3 KG) PICKLED HAM HOCK
2 CLOVES GARLIC, PEELED
SALT
1 MEDIUM YELLOW ONION, DICED

BASE AND TOPPINGS

16 TORTILLAS (PAGE 66)
VARIOUS SALSAS (PAGES 50–53 AND 68–69)

Heat a large pot over medium heat. Fry the bacon in the pot for about 10 minutes. It should produce a lot of grease. Add the lard and, as soon as it melts, add the oil.

Crush the peppercorns in a mortar and pestle and combine the bay leaves, smoked paprika, dried bell pepper, dried chile peppers, marjoram, cumin, and oregano to make a rub. Rub the ham hock thoroughly, saving any of the rub that doesn't stick. Place the meat in the oil and add the leftover rub and the garlic cloves to the pot. Decrease the heat so that the oil bubbles very gently. Now you'll have to wait 3 hours, while turning the ham hock every half hour. Remove the pork from the oil and drain it in a colander for 5 minutes. Then transfer it to a large cutting board and separate the meat from the bone using a meat cleaver (if you don't have a cleaver, use a kitchen knife). Chop the pork, including the fat and rind, into small pieces. Season it with a little salt and distribute it on the tortillas with a little diced onion, nothing more!

LAMB TACOS
WITH HUMMUS, POMEGRANATE SEEDS, AND MINT YOGURT

SERVES 2

FUSION TORTILLAS

1¼ CUPS (150 G) HARINA DE MAIZ (FINE NIXTAMALIZED CORNMEAL)

1 TEASPOON HARISSA

1 TEASPOON PAPRIKA

⅓ CUP (80 ML) WATER

½ TEASPOON SALT

VEGETABLE OIL, FOR FRYING

FILLING

12 OUNCES LAMB STEAKS

4 TABLESPOONS OLIVE OIL

½ TEASPOON HARISSA

FRESHLY GROUND BLACK PEPPER

1 CLOVE GARLIC, MINCED

⅔ CUP (150 G) HUMMUS

⅔ CUP (150 G) PLAIN YOGURT

SEEDS FROM 1 POMEGRANATE

1 BUNCH MINT, LEAVES SHREDDED

SALT

JUICE OF 2 LIMES

Prepare the tortillas as described on page 66 using the ingredients listed above and wrap them in a kitchen towel to keep them warm.

To make the filling, cut the lamb steaks into small cubes and rub them with 2 tablespoons of the olive oil, the harissa, and pepper.

Heat the remaining 2 tablespoons olive oil in a skillet over high heat and sear the lamb. Don't cook it for more than 3 to 4 minutes or it will become too tough. After about 2 minutes, add the garlic.

Remove the lamb from the pan. Spread each tortilla with 1 tablespoon hummus and distribute the lamb evenly over the top. Top each taco with 1 tablespoon yogurt and sprinkle with pomegranate seeds and a few shredded mint leaves. Last of all, season with salt and pepper and drizzle with a little lime juice. Your Moroccan taco fusion is now ready.

ASIAN TACOS

SERVES 2

BASE
8 TORTILLAS (PAGE 66)

FILLING
HANDFUL OF BABY GREEN ASPARAGUS
VEGETABLE OIL
JUICE OF 2 LIMES
12 OUNCES (340 G) BEEF SIRLOIN STEAKS
1 CLOVE GARLIC, MINCED
1 RED CHILE PEPPER, SEEDED AND CHOPPED
1/3 INCH (1 CM) FRESH GINGER, MINCED
9 TABLESPOONS SOY SAUCE OR NICA SAUCE
(PAGE 52)
4 RADISHES, SLICED, FOR GARNISH
WATERCRESS, FOR GARNISH
FRESHLY GROUND BLACK PEPPER

To make the filling, remove the woody ends of the asparagus, and cut the asparagus into small pieces. Heat a little vegetable oil in a skillet over medium heat and sear the asparagus for 7 to 12 minutes, until the pieces are golden brown. Remove it from the pan, drizzle it with half of the juice of 1 lime, and set aside.

Cut the steaks into strips about 1/3 inch (1 cm) thick and sear them in vegetable oil for no more than 20 seconds on each side so that they stay nice and pink inside. Add the garlic, chile, and ginger, followed by the soy sauce, and stir to combine.

Fill each taco with meat, several asparagus spears, radishes, and watercress. Finish them off with a squeeze of lime juice and pepper—and serve away!

SCALLOP TACOS

SERVES 2

BASE
8 SEPIA-TORTILLAS
(PAGE 67)

FILLING
8 MEDIUM SCALLOPS
VEGETABLE OIL
2 CLOVES GARLIC, MINCED
½ RED CHILE PEPPER, SEEDED AND MINCED
5 OUNCES (150 ML) WHITE WINE
2 TABLESPOONS FRESH CILANTRO LEAVES, CHOPPED
2 HANDFULS LAMB'S LETTUCE
1 MANGO, PEELED AND DICED
⅔ CUP (150 G) CRÈME FRAÎCHE
1 LIME, SLICED INTO 8 WEDGES
SALT AND FRESHLY GROUND BLACK PEPPER

To prepare the filling, heat a little oil in a skillet over high heat. Brown the scallops until both sides are golden, 2 to 4 minutes for each side, add the garlic and chile pepper. Pour in the white wine. Let the alcohol evaporate for 30 seconds, then sprinkle in the cilantro, stir briefly, and let stand for another 30 seconds.

Cover each tortilla with a bed of lamb's lettuce and top with some mango and a dollop of crème fraîche. Remove the scallops from the sauce, cut them into bite-size pieces, and arrange them on each of the tortillas. Drizzle each taco with 1 to 2 tablespoons cilantro–white wine sauce, squeeze a lime wedge over the top, and season them with lots of salt and pepper.

LOOKING FOR TROUBLE

When we travel, we'd much rather bring home tattoos than souvenirs. When we asked where we could find the best tattoos in Guadalajara, we were sent to Erick Cuevas. (You'll find him on Instagram under "imtheraptor.") Erick added several outstanding pieces to our existing tattoo collections. Cozy decided to have "Salt & Silver" tattooed on his neck—brilliant! Both of us added the phrase "Rock around the clock." I (Jo) decided to start a set of kitchen herbs, beginning with a sprig of sage. Erick also worked on the fish collection on my forearm, adding an angelfish like the one I used to keep in an aquarium. Our thirst for ink was satisfied—for a while, anyway. A few days later we learned about an excellent old-school tattoo artist named Pedro Snake, so we had to visit him, too. Cozy had him add some kitchen appliances on his leg—a nice wooden mortar and a blender to start. This time Jo made do with a small espresso cup below the knee.

But we had something else in common with Erick, too: graffiti. He introduced us to several artists from the EYOA crew. We waited until dark so we could all go painting together, and we brought along the camera to take pictures. At first everything went smoothly, no vandalism. But just as we were finishing a huge, complex picture on the wall of an old warehouse, someone wrote his tag on a rusty front door to a house—not a very good idea. We heard someone quickly turning a key in the lock, and we scrammed. There was anger bellow-ing behind us. One glance over the shoulder gave us a further burst of energy and a rush of adrenaline. We were being chased by an angry mob of Mexicans, some carrying machetes. It looked like our friend had tagged the wrong door!

We ran as fast as our legs could carry us, turning a few corners, literally running for our lives. Then we split up. While I sprinted into a small dark alley to the right, Cozy and Erick veered left. I was alone. About 330 feet (100 meters) before the next intersection, I spotted the red and blue flashing lights of a squad car reflected on the walls. I dove out of range of a streetlamp and rolled underneath a pickup truck just as the police car came around the corner. I didn't know if I'd been seen. The police car crawled slowly up the street in my direction. Lying under the truck, I pulled my hood down over my face and fumbled to remove the memory card from the camera—to eliminate any evidence and to save the photos if I hap-pened to be searched. I tried to breathe as quietly as pos-sible, even though I was completely out of breath. My lungs were burning. I hid the memory card by the curb beside me between some cigarette butts and an old cola can. Shit, the car was slowing down even more. It finally came to a stop right next to the truck. The cops got out. I saw only their leather boots, navy blue cargo pants, and the dangling barrel of a shotgun. Holy shit. The police talked quietly among themselves in Spanish. I under-stood only so much. They were looking for us. The way

Europe who had to get to the airport the next morning, and heads would roll if anything happened to him. The policemen didn't buy it and just kept leading them

When we woke up the next morning, we both agreed that it was time to move on. We'd had enough of the city—the ocean was calling! But we'd learned one thing, at least:

BYE-BYE, GUADALAJARA!

SAN PANCHO
NAYARIT

We arrived in San Pancho, a small surfer spot in the state of Nayarit, on an extremely hot, off-season afternoon. The place was deserted. The shutters on the businesses were all closed up and there wasn't a soul on the dusty village road to the ocean. All that was missing were vultures circling over our heads. What did people do in such a godforsaken town? Finally we discovered an open store, the Santa Madre Surf Co. Bingo! We opened the door and walked in. Two guys around our age sat behind the counter staring at a laptop covered in surf stickers. "*Ahuevo!*" one of them said. He had short, black hair and a single red dreadlock at the back of his head. "*No mames!*" replied the other. We didn't understand a word. Suddenly they noticed us, looked at us with blank stares, and asked if we had boards. We said we did. We started to introduce ourselves, but the two of them weren't big on formalities. Their

Luigi, Dess, Pablo

names were Pablo and Luigi, and they'd just learned that
there were supposed to be good waves at a spot nearby.
They abruptly closed up shop, and we threw our boards
into an old Japanese station wagon and headed for the
waves. Pablo rolled a joint. The tape deck was playing
Bob Marley as we drove to a spot called La Lancha. The
wave was breaking right next to a giant luxury resort
surrounded by a tall barbed-wire fence. At the gate stood
armed guards who were only letting people through if
they had surfboards. In Mexico, luxury resorts are sealed
off and heavily guarded so that the tourist groups can
feel safe. At some point, however, the local surfers had
managed to make a deal with the guards: Anyone with
a surfboard could enter. Nevertheless, the guards wrote
down our vehicle's license plate number as well as our
exact arrival time and group number, so that they could
keep track of how many people entered the premises. We
followed a narrow path through jungle and undergrowth
that led to the beach. There we found crystal-clear, turquoise-blue water and perfect two-meter waves—our best
start ever!

MEXICO SURF GUIDE // PART I
NAYARIT

Luigi from the Santa Madre Surf Co. was nice enough to write a guide to his favorite spots in the Bahía de Banderas.

SAN PANCHO 20.89879°N -105.41807°E

Here you'll find a fast left that starts at the southern end of the main beach and has a steep barrel section at the river mouth. This wave gets as high as 10 feet (3 meters). The surfing is best when there's a northwest swell, as there usually is in winter, but sometimes you'll find the biggest waves after the summer rainy season, when there's a typical southwest swell. The waves are best at mid to low tide.

To get there, just follow the main road from San Pancho along the beach. Mornings are pretty dead, so that's the best time to go. But the most beautiful time is just before sunset, and the place is pretty dead at that time, too.

SAN PANCHO

LA LANCHA 20.74785°N −105.44167°E

This beautiful beach with white sand and coral reefs is accessible only via private property. You can't get there on a surfboard; you can only get there on foot, by car, or by boat. On foot, it's a forty-minute walk over rocks to the southern end of Punta de Mita.

The blaze of color and the crystal-clear water make this point break a paradise. Because it's somewhat remote, you'll often see wildlife, such as turtles and dolphins. But when we were there, there was trouble in paradise: Near the spot where the waves were breaking, we saw a baby dolphin. Several surfers swam toward it but it was already dead. We pulled it out of the water and held a small burial ceremony. All the surfers were really bummed, but we also came to believe that the baby dolphin had magical powers: That day the waves hadn't been very good, but after we buried the dolphin, they were suddenly super and we all had a great afternoon. When it was over, we thanked the baby dolphin for the good waves.

BURROS 20.75132°N −105.45922°E

This is Luigi's favorite spot in the entire area. The waves come from almost every direction, but the best come from the northwest in winter. In the summer, the good waves come from the southwest. Rights for longboards and shortboards are best surfed at high tide. The way to the beach is a five-minute walk through jungle along a stony creek that ends at a surprisingly stony beach. Unfortunately it's pretty crowded on the weekends!

CÓCTELS TÉ
TEA COCKTAILS

When we got back to San Pancho after our surf session, the town had woken up from its siesta. There were grills on the streets, traditional Mexican banda music playing in the clubs, and lots of color and movement. We went with Pablo and Luigi to Darjeeling, a favorite surfer bar in San Pancho that served a drink we just had to share with you: *coctel té*. It's made up of several types of home-mixed teas that are freshly brewed, chilled with ice cubes, and then mixed with alcohol, fruit juices, and honey. There's nothing better for discussing the day's best waves than a fresh *coctel té*. Try it!

RED BERRY TEA WITH VODKA

SERVES 1

1 TEASPOON LOOSE RED BERRY TEA

1 TEASPOON HONEY

1 TABLESPOON LIME JUICE

1 TO 3 TABLESPOONS VODKA

ICE CUBES

Place the tea in a strainer in a serving cup, pour 1/3 cup (80 ml) boiling water over it, and let steep for 10 minutes.

Remove the strainer and stir in the honey and lime juice. Add 1/2 cup (120 ml) cold water and fill the cup almost to the top with ice cubes. Then add the vodka, stir, and drink.

ROOIBOS TEA WITH SCOTCH

SERVES 1

1 TABLESPOON LOOSE ROOIBOS TEA

2 TEASPOONS LIGHT BROWN SUGAR

PINCH OF UNSWEETENED COCOA POWDER

1 TO 3 TABLESPOONS SCOTCH

ICE CUBES

Place the tea in a strainer in a serving cup, pour 1/3 cup (80 ml) boiling water over it, and let steep for 10 minutes.

Remove the strainer and stir in the sugar and cocoa powder. Add 1/2 cup (120 ml) cold water and fill the cup almost to the top with ice cubes. Then add the Scotch, stir, and drink.

FAST FOOD

BLACK TEA WITH TEQUILA

SERVES 1

1 TEASPOON LOOSE BLACK TEA
1 TABLESPOON LOOSE FRUIT TEA OF YOUR CHOICE
2 TEASPOONS HONEY
1 TABLESPOON LIME JUICE
1/2 INCH ORANGE PEEL
1 TO 3 TABLESPOONS WHITE TEQUILA

Place both types of tea in a strainer in a serving cup, pour 1/3 cup (80 ml) boiling water over them, and let steep for 10 minutes.

Remove the strainer. Stir in the honey, lime juice, and orange peel. Add 1/2 cup (120 ml) cold water and fill the cup almost to the top with ice cubes. Then add the tequila, stir, and drink.

GREEN TEA WITH RUM

SERVES 1

1 TEASPOON LOOSE GREEN TEA
5 DRIED PINEAPPLE RINGS, CUT AS NEEDED
3 TEASPOONS MAPLE SYRUP
1 TO 3 TABLESPOONS RUM
SEVERAL FRESH MINT LEAVES, FOR GARNISH
1/2 TEASPOON FRESH MARIGOLD FLOWERS, FOR GARNISH

Place the tea and pineapple rings in a strainer in a serving cup; pour 1/2 cup (120 ml) boiling water over them, and let steep for 10 minutes.

Remove the strainer. Stir in the maple syrup. Add 1/2 cup (120 ml) cold water and fill the cup almost to the top with ice cubes. Then add the rum, stir, garnish with mint leaves and marigold flowers, and drink.

FRUIT TEA WITH BATIDA DE COCO

SERVES 1

1 TABLESPOON LOOSE FRUIT TEA OF YOUR CHOICE
1 TEASPOON MAPLE SYRUP
1 TEASPOON LEMON JUICE
1 TEASPOON GROUND HAZELNUTS
PINCH OF GROUND CINNAMON
1 TABLESPOON SOY MILK
3 TABLESPOONS BATIDA DE COCO

Place the tea in a strainer in a serving cup, pour 1/3 cup (80 ml) boiling water over it, and let steep for 10 minutes.

Remove the strainer. Stir in the maple syrup, lemon juice, hazelnuts, and cinnamon. Add 1/2 cup (120 ml) cold water and the soy milk, and fill the cup almost to the top with ice cubes. Then add the batida de coco, stir, and drink.

PORTOBELLO-SHRIMP BURGERS

The Darjeeling also had a kitchen, where we met Memo, a surfer, sailboat captain, and truly gifted chef. He made us this fantastic burger.

MAKES 2 BURGERS

1 TABLESPOON UNSALTED BUTTER
2 LARGE PORTOBELLO MUSHROOMS
2 CHEESE SLICES (STILTON WORKS WELL)
OLIVE OIL, FOR FRYING
2 HANDFULS PEELED MEDIUM SHRIMP
JUICE OF 1 LIME
SALT
1 TO 2 TABLESPOONS MAYONNAISE
(PAGE 51)

½ TEASPOON RED PEPPER FLAKES
FRESHLY GROUND BLACK PEPPER
2 HAMBURGER BUNS
GREEN LEAF LETTUCE LEAVES
1 TOMATO, THINLY SLICED
1 SMALL RED ONION, SLICED INTO
THIN RINGS
CHIPOTLE-LIME SAUCE (PAGE 51),
FOR SERVING

Melt the butter in an ovenproof pan. When it starts to bubble, add the portobellos and broil them for about 5 minutes on each side. Top the portobellos with the cheese and broil them until the cheese is melted and golden brown.

While the mushrooms are broiling, heat the oil in a second pan over high heat. Add the shrimp and fry them for 4 to 5 minutes, until they're nice and pink. Pour half the lime juice over the shrimp and season with salt. Mix together the remaining lime juice with the mayonnaise and red pepper flakes. Season with pepper.

Cut the hamburger buns in half crosswise and toast the cut sides briefly. Spread them with a little seasoned mayo and stack the other ingredients on top of the bottom halves: first the lettuce, then the mushrooms, then shrimp, tomato slices, onion rings, and, finally, a dollop of the Chipotle-Lime Sauce. Cover with the top bun halves.

VEGGIE

SANTA MADRES WAVECRUSHERS

Every Saturday, there was a hippie market in San Pancho where people sold homemade blonde wigs and other interesting things. Our favorites were the large selection of home-roasted coffee blends, fantastic street food, and homegrown tomatoes. Luigi and Pablo earned a little money selling homemade smoothies. We had to repair two of their surfboards and clean their entire apartment before they would share these brilliant recipes with us.

For all the smoothies: Prepare all the ingredients as necessary (peel, remove seeds, and so on), place them in a blender, and blend on high speed. Then add 2 ice cubes. Each recipe serves 1 to 2.

RED
1 LARGE BEET, PEELED AND COOKED
HANDFUL OF BLUEBERRIES
1 RHUBARB STALK, COOKED
1 RED APPLE
3/4 CUP (180 ML) COLD ROSEHIP TEA

ORANGE
1 MANGO
3 PEACHES
1 1/2 INCHES (4 CM) FRESH GINGER
1 CARROT
3/4 CUP (180 ML) ORANGE JUICE

YELLOW
1 BANANA
1 STAR FRUIT
1/4 HONEYDEW MELON
1/2 MANGO
10 FRESH MINT LEAVES
1/2 CUP (120 ML) PINEAPPLE JUICE
1 1/4 CUPS (300 ML) WATER

GREEN
1 KIWI
2 HANDFULS WHITE GRAPES
1 PEAR
HANDFUL OF SPINACH
HANDFUL OF CILANTRO
1/4 AVOCADO
3/4 CUP (180 ML) APPLE JUICE
1/2 CUP (120 ML) WATER

BROWN
1 BANANA
1 SWEET PEAR
HANDFUL OF PLAIN BISCOTTI
1/2 CUP (120 ML) ALMOND MILK
3/4 CUP (180 ML) WHOLE MILK
1 BREWED ESPRESSO

We partied. The vibe in San Pancho was so laid back that we just couldn't tear ourselves away. It got to where we knew everyone in the village and never missed a party or a surf session. With our new friends, we visited secret beaches, crashed the pools at million-dollar villas in the middle of the night, and slept here, there, and everywhere. Our home base was Luigi and Pablo's place, though it was constantly filled with other guests from Guadalajara—which meant that we often ended up in the hammocks or had to sleep on our surf bags. During the Semana Santa (Holy Week) at Eastertime, San Pancho went wild. The usually sleepy little village suddenly woke up big time.

The entire beach was covered with the tents of Mexican families who had come for Easter vacation. It was like one gigantic festival, and our local friends took advantage of the opportunity to earn as much money as possible in anticipation of the leaner off-season times. We did whatever we could, helping Pablo roll sushi to sell on the beach, teaching kids to surf with Luigi. We celebrated so insanely in the evenings after work that it was a miracle we weren't killed attempting a drunken backward somersault from the roof of a house into a tiny pool. We tried to compensate for our unhealthy lifestyle with yoga lessons from Pauly. The whole gang took Dess's enormous SUV for a surf trip and spent weeks in the country.

After a while, we came up with the brilliant idea of buying a car for our future travels. We found one that we really liked: a gigantic 1985 Ford Club Wagon with a V8 engine, bed, and sound system, absolutely insane. The owner, who was also a surfer, claimed that the car was in top condition and would easily carry us to the ends of the earth. We agreed to buy it but told him we wouldn't pay until a mechanic had given it a thorough going-over. We spruced it up a little, repainted it, and took it to a mechanic who was recommended by a friend. The mechanic was a bug-eyed old bomber covered from head to toe in motor oil, with long gray hair sticking out in every direction. Our kind of guy. For a small fee, he agreed to examine our clunker. When we came back the next day, he cheerfully babbled on and on—not always comprehensibly—and confirmed that the car was in top shape; he just had to replace a part on the clutch. We gave him a little money for the part and came back two days later.

A bad moment: Our new mechanic explains that our car is a piece of junk.

This time he was lying underneath the car and had removed half the engine. He claimed that as he was working on it, he'd found two or three other little problems that needed fixing so that the car would guzzle less gas and would start reliably. We were skeptical at first and suspected that he was trying to squeeze a little more money out of us, but he showed us so many broken parts that we finally gave in. Besides, we were planning on driving it all the way to Chile, so we needed it to be in the best shape possible. We gave him another 90 euros (about $100) and another week to work on it. We weren't in any hurry. The sun was shining, the food was great, and the waves were big. We had a few relaxing days and returned to the shop a week later. The car had been reassembled. After two attempts at starting it, the engine coughed to life. We seated Sergio the mechanic—who had meanwhile become a friend—in the passenger seat and took a test drive. The car ran perfectly and we were thrilled, cruising through the city with the music turned up full blast. When we'd almost completed our little circuit, just about a thousand feet (300 meters) from the shop, the engine backfired twice, gave a tired sigh, and died. Sergio babbled something to himself, rubbed his hair, and jumped out of the car. He had foam at the corners of his mouth and was grinding his teeth. He seemed a little crazy. We pushed the car back to the shop, gave him two more days and another 45 euros ($50), and hoped for a miracle. His shop was right next door to the local police station, which we took to be a good sign and felt a little better.

When we came back two days later, accompanied by the friend who had recommended him, Sergio had completely disappeared. Our car was still there, but in pieces. We tried to ask the cops next door what had happened to Sergio, but they were already grinning at us before we'd said a word. Slurping their colas, they asked if we hadn't noticed how Sergio was spending all our money on crystal meth instead of car parts. Then they sent us on our way, laughing, with a friendly "Piss off, gringos."

We called our friend Dess, who came and picked us up in her SUV. She seemed angrier at the situation than we were, to the point where she completely lost it. She jumped out of her car, stormed into the shop, and screamed at the workers until they told her where Sergio lived. It must not have been far, because Dess steamed out of the shop like a runaway locomotive headed straight for some old shacks. She walked up to a door, hammered on it with her fists, and bellowed out some wild Mexican curses. Then she picked up a rock and threw it at a dusty windowpane. When she looked through the hole and saw Sergio trying to hide, she took a run at the rickety door and broke it in. Sergio was standing in the corner, wide-eyed and in his underwear, and had no idea what was happening to him. "Gimme the money!" Dess barked. He had only 18 euros (about $20) of our money left, which he gave us with a whimper. Tough girl, our Dess! And she's only 5 feet 2 inches tall. We took our measly euros and walked back to Dess's car.

Dess had a friend tow our car to a qualified mechanic, who checked it out in our presence and confirmed what the cops had already told us: Absolutely nothing had been fixed. All Sergio had done was tape two magnets to the gas line as a fuel-saving measure. The new mechanic told us our car was totally worthless and if we were lucky, we might get a couple hundred euros for the scrap metal. Brokenhearted, we abandoned our monster truck. At least we hadn't paid the owner the 2,800 euros ($3,100) he was asking for it. He could reassemble the bucket of bolts himself. Our new mechanic friend, Abdel, took us to a used-car market where, for 900 euros ($1,000), we bought a supercool 1996 Chevy SUV. Abdel installed a roof rack, and we were finally on our way south. It was high time, too. Our next stop was Pascuales, near Tecomán, and then we would continue on to La Ticla in Michoacán.

Our friend Dess, who reduced a Mexican mechanic
to a whimpering blob all by herself.

We're finally on our way.
C U later, San Pancho!

MEXICO SURF GUIDE // PART II
COLIMA

PASCUALES 18.85516°N -103.96191°E

Only eight minutes from Tecomán, there's a valley of the same name with a thousand palm trees waving in the breeze where you'll find monster barrels. Your best bet is to go straight to Shaper—the guy who owns the guest-house on the beach—to get the right board.

The waves here crash onto flat sandbanks, practically unobstructed. If you're lucky you'll find a solid southern swell.

Jesus!!! That was my first thought when we arrived in Pascuales. Pascuales is a Mexican surf spot known for its enormous, raw, high-speed waves that break over black sand and can reach heights of up to 32 feet (10 meters). On especially good days, it's populated with pro surfers and rescue teams on jet skis. On the windy day when we arrived in Pascuales, the waves were "only" about 13 feet (4 meters) high, but they were still the biggest and most difficult we'd ever paddled into.

I stood on the beach for about an hour trying to figure out the best end from which to enter this chaos. I finally gathered up my courage and paddled out into the water. Unfortunately, my strategy didn't quite work out the way I wanted. I hadn't even gone 65 feet (20 meters) when, within seconds, the current had carried me over 650 feet (200 meters) down the beach, straight into the steep peaks I'd been trying to avoid. I was hopeful that I'd be able to escape during a quieter phase between sets, but a menacing black line suddenly appeared on the horizon. I paddled as fast as I could in the direction of the wall of water as it rolled toward me. I was still hoping I'd be fast enough to escape it before it broke over me. But no, the first wave in this freak set broke exactly 32 feet (10 meters) in front of me, putting me in the worst possible position. There was no chance of a duck dive; by the time the wall of white foam reached me, it was twice my height. I let go of my board and dove down as far as my leash allowed to keep from being sucked into the most danger-ous section. But this wave was much too heavy for me to escape so easily. When the water hit me, it felt like I'd been thrown into an enormous, angry washing machine. I had no idea how far I was below the surface, or which way was up, or how fast the time was passing. How long was I underwater? I'd say it was about as long as it took me to recite the Ave Maria in my head.

When I opened my eyes, everything was black. The surface was nowhere in sight. All I could do was to stay calm and try not to fight against the wave until it let go of me. That's not so easy when your lungs are running out of oxygen. At the last possible moment, just as I was about to start swallowing water, it got lighter and the swirling became less powerful. I frantically paddled in the direction I thought was up. Later my friends told me I shot out of the foam like a cork out of a Champagne bottle. Air!

Unfortunately, however...that was only the first of three waves. When I came up for air after the third, I suddenly had a brilliant idea: I would get out of the water, have myself a beer and some *aguachile*, and put off my next attempt until the next day.

AGUACHILE
SPICY SHRIMP COCKTAIL

This Mexican beach classic is normally prepared like ceviche (page 176), using raw shrimp. But since the raw shrimp we find at home is rarely fresh enough, we prefer to precook them. *Aguachile* tastes best on hot summer days—and especially on hot summer days at the beach.

MEXICO

SERVES 2

MARINADE
¼ CUCUMBER
½ CLOVE GARLIC
1 BUNCH CILANTRO
1 CUP (240 ML) LIME JUICE (ABOUT 6 LIMES)
¼ CUP (60 ML) OLIVE OIL
3 SMALL CHILE PEPPERS
SEA SALT

1 POUND (500 G) PEELED MEDIUM SHRIMP
1 MEDIUM RED ONION, SLICED INTO RINGS
½ CUCUMBER, SLICED INTO ¼-INCH-THICK
(½ CM) COINS

For the marinade, peel and cut the cucumber into quarters. Then put it in a blender along with the garlic, cilantro, lime juice, olive oil, chile peppers, and sea salt, and blend them into a sauce.

Bring a pot of water to a boil, and cook the shrimp in the boiling water for 2 minutes. Transfer the shrimp to a bowl, add the onion and cucumber slices, and pour the marinade over the top. Let this mixture sit with the marinade for about 30 minutes before eating.

MEXICO SURF GUIDE // PART III
MICHOACÁN

LA TICLA 18.45425°N -103.55983°E

This is an unbelievably beautiful spot that should not be missed. La Ticla is also called Garanticla, because it guarantees good conditions for surfers. Every year surfers come from around the world to experience the power of these waves. There are rights and lefts for all types of surfboards. The best surfing conditions are to be found during the summer when offshore winds are blowing from the northwest and an ideal swell is approaching from the south. Here you're independent of the tides. But watch out for sea urchins and rocks! La Ticla is busy almost year-round.

You can either rent a small bungalow or, as we did, pay 2.75 euros (about $3) a night for a hammock in a *hamaquera*, a simple hut. They even have electricity, showers, and toilets. What more could you want?

RIO NEXPA 18.08552°N -102.79113°E

This point break is famous for its massive left barrels. Unfortunately, we spent only two nights here, but we had a solid swell with 10-foot (3-meter) faces. This spot is well-known, and there's lots of traffic in the water, but you'll also find accommodations to suit any budget. It's definitely worth a visit!

RIO NEXPA BBQ
NEXPA RIVER BARBECUE

We rushed to buy out the entire stock of the last open market and then headed straight back to the beach. The next perfect Pacific wave and the next grilling session were calling. One of our favorite snacks in Mexico was grilled pineapple slices with chile and limes, so we added them to this recipe, too!

SERVES 8

3¹⁄₃ POUNDS (1½ KG) BEEF TENDERLOIN

MARINADE
¹⁄₃ CUP (80 ML) DARK MALT BEER
¹⁄₄ CUP (60 ML) OLIVE OIL
1 TABLESPOON HONEY
6 CLOVES GARLIC
1 TEASPOON WHOLE BLACK PEPPERCORNS

VEGETABLES
4 LARGE RUSSET POTATOES
4 SWEET POTATOES
2 LARGE ZUCCHINI
2 SMALL EGGPLANTS
1 TABLESPOON LIGHT BROWN SUGAR
4 TABLESPOONS UNSALTED BUTTER
1³⁄₄ TABLESPOONS OLIVE OIL
JUICE OF 1 TO 2 LIMES
COARSE SEA SALT AND FRESHLY GROUND
BLACK PEPPER
1 BUNCH CILANTRO
1 PINEAPPLE
1 TEASPOON CHILI POWDER

To prepare the meat, cut the beef across the grain into ¹⁄₃-inch-thick (1 cm) slices. For the marinade, vigorously whisk together the soy sauce, beer, olive oil, and honey. Place the beef in a plastic container. Add the marinade and slosh the meat around in it. Crush the unpeeled garlic cloves with the handle of a large knife, crush the peppercorns, and add both to the container. Refrigerate the beef for at least 2 hours (or even better, overnight) so that the marinade can really soak into the beef.

Preheat the grill to high heat. To prepare the vegetables, cut each of them into four equal-size pieces. Bring a pot of salted water to a boil. As soon as the water boils, decrease the heat and add the russet potatoes. After 10 minutes, add the sweet potatoes. After another 15 minutes, add the zucchini and eggplant and boil for 10 more minutes. Drain the vegetables in a colander and set them aside.

Place the vegetables on the grill grate and sprinkle them with the brown sugar. The sugar will caramelize and gives the vegetables a sweet, smoky taste. Because you precooked the vegetables, they'll need only a few minutes on each side till they're crisp on the outside and tender on the inside!

Once the vegetables have developed a nice crust, transfer them to a large bowl. Melt the butter in a small saucepan, whisk it with the olive oil and lime juice, and season it with a lot of salt and pepper. Pour this dressing over the vegetables. Chop the cilantro coarsely and sprinkle it on top, then mix everything together well.

Peel and cut the pineapple into thick slices and grill it for 2 minutes on each side so that it caramelizes around the edges. Then season it with chili powder, salt, and a little lime juice.

Now your grill should be very hot. That's important, because the beef really needs to start sizzling as soon as it hits the rack. Drain the meat from the marinade and sear it on the hottest part of the grill for 30 seconds on each side. At the right hot temperature, the meat stays tender and pink inside while the outside acquires an authentic grilled f lavor. Of course, you can also have your steak

well-done, but that's not how we like it. Remove it from the grill, season it with lots of salt and pepper, and serve it with the vegetables. Bon appétit!

The only photo we secretly didn't delete.

MICHOACÁN

Before we left San Pancho for parts farther south, we were warned over and over again not to drive through Michoacán. We were even advised to make a wide, daylong detour around it, through the interior. As is so often the case in Mexico, it all had to do with the war with the drug cartels. For several years, the Knights Templar cartel had maintained a reign of terror in Michoacán, which gave rise to vigilante groups. Our friends described the situation as follows: The cartel's heavily armed henchmen would drive an armada of pickup trucks into the villages and cities and help themselves to anything they wanted, extort protection money from peasants and small shop owners, and abduct women. The civilian population rose up in protest, initially led by a teacher. In numerous bloody encounters with the Knights Templar, this vigilante army had managed to reclaim most of the state. Ignoring all the warnings and deciding to see for ourselves, we took off through Michoacán.

The street scene changed dramatically when we left the state of Jalisco and drove the first 1¼ miles (2 kilometers) into Michoacán. Just before each town, the road was lined with rocks, sandbags, and barbed wire. The entrances to the towns were like fortresses; the stories about civil war were apparently true. As we approached each town, we crossed *topes* (speed bumps) at a crawl. Behind the barriers were groups of heavily armed villagers with walkie-talkies. We saw old AK-47 assault rifles, shotguns, revolvers—these guys meant business! Our hearts beat a little faster than usual as we passed through the first town. The guards examined us closely. We said hello and they nodded back. Their looks were stone cold, but they let us pass undisturbed. The surfboards on the car roof and our European appearance seemed enough to convince the locals that we posed no threat. At the other end of town, we found a similar scene. The guards had evidently been informed of our arrival via walkie-talkies and ignored us. They were lounging on plastic chairs, drinking beer, with their weapons leaning against a fruit stand. Siesta.

On the long stretches between towns, we were constantly meeting convoys of military vehicles, complete with hooded soldiers on the truck beds and machine guns on the roofs. Scary. After we'd driven through several checkpoints and gradually gotten used to the constant surveillance of peasants armed to the teeth, we started to get itchy fingers—itchy picture-taking fingers, that is. I whipped out the camera as Cozy steered the car toward the next town entrance. Cranking down the side window, I aimed the camera at the checkpoint. It was fine—until it wasn't.

When the sleepy guard saw the camera, he suddenly came to life. Frantic commands were issued and everybody jumped out of their chairs, waving their weapons. We suddenly realized that taking pictures wasn't such a clever idea after all. Before we knew it, our car was surrounded by gun barrels. The leader of the band came to the passenger window and shouted questions at us: Who were we, what did we want, who were the pictures for? I put on my friendliest smile and explained that we were just two surfers from Europe taking a few vacation photos. As I spoke, I turned on the camera and showed him a few nice surfing shots, hoping he wouldn't confiscate all our equipment. He ordered me to delete all the pictures I'd just taken of the checkpoint. As he watched, I reluctantly pressed the "delete" button until all the photos of armed militia had been erased. Meanwhile, I excused myself a thousand times and explained that we really hadn't had any bad intentions. Someone yelled that they should take our camera as a precaution. Someone else yelled that they should confiscate our whole car. Next came a brief but heated discussion, during which the guns stayed pointed at us, and our car. We couldn't make out much of what they were saying, but in the end it was obvious that the patron saint of travelers was on our side. The leader of the group had his way, and we were allowed to keep our camera. But he warned us not to film or photograph any of the vigilantes because the pictures could fall into the hands of the cartel and put these people in danger. Despite the grumbled objections of the other cowboys, he sent us on our way. We didn't have to be told twice—we beat it!

CAFÉ DE OLLA
SPICED MEXICAN COFFEE

What could be better than a hot, spiced Mexican coffee at dawn just before the day's first surf session? We highly recommend it. We quickly added this ritual to our standard surf trip repertoire. Even if you're in the middle of nowhere, heat water on the coals left from the previous night's campfire and pour it through a bandanna or a piece of cloth instead of a filter. This coffee will give you the perfect start to your day. We know from experience.

SERVES 1

¼ CUP (50 G) BROWN CANE SUGAR
1 CINNAMON STICK
5 WHOLE CLOVES
PEEL FROM ½ ORANGE
¼ CUP (60 G) COARSELY GROUND COFFEE

In a pot, combine the sugar, cinnamon stick, cloves, orange peel, and 4 cups (1 liter) water and simmer for 5 minutes. Add the coffee and bring it to a boil. Remove the pot from the heat, cover it, and let the coffee brew for 5 minutes. Pour the coffee through a fine strainer (or a bandanna or piece of cloth). Drink, wax your board, and surf.

PEDRO POLAKO'S PERFECT BBQ RIBS

On a deserted beach, there's nothing better to do than have a decadent grilling session. On Jo's birthday, our Polish beach buddy Pedro surprised us with this gem: perfect barbecued ribs. They take a while to prepare, but we swear it's worth it. If you ever want to serve something truly extraordinary at your barbecue, then treat yourself and your friends to these juicy, smoky ribs.

SERVES 6

RIBS
6½ POUNDS (3 KG) BEEF RIBS

BRINE
1 CUP (200 G) SUGAR
2/3 CUP (200 G) SALT
5 BAY LEAVES
SEVERAL DRIED HERBS OF YOUR CHOICE
(SUCH AS MARJORAM, OREGANO, OR
OTHER HERBS WITH AN EARTHY AROMA)

BARBECUE SAUCE
5 CUPS KETCHUP
2 CUPS (480 ML) SUGAR BEET SYRUP
1½ CUPS (360 ML) APPLE CIDER VINEGAR
1 2/3 CUPS (350 G) DARK BROWN SUGAR
3 TEASPOONS ONION POWDER
2 TEASPOONS GARLIC POWDER
2 TEASPOONS VINEGAR POWDER
(AVAILABLE IN ASIAN MARKETS)
1 TEASPOON CAYENNE PEPPER

DRY RUB
2½ TEASPOONS DRIED MARJORAM
2½ TEASPOONS FRESHLY GROUND
BLACK PEPPER
1 TEASPOON SALT

Rinse the ribs in cold water and pat them dry with paper towels. Remove any excess fat and—very important—remove the paper-thin membrane on the inside of the ribs. Because you want to prepare the ribs PERFECTLY, you first need to soak them in brine.

To make the brine, combine all the ingredients plus about 6 cups (1.5 liters) water in a large pot and heat until the sugar and salt have dissolved. Let the brine cool. Place the ribs in the brine and soak them for the desired period—they can easily stay in there for 5 to 12 hours in the refrigerator. This gives the meat an especially intense flavor.

To make the barbecue sauce, combine all of the ingredients in a large pot and reduce over low heat for 2 to 3 hours, stirring occasionally. Then let the sauce cool.

For the dry rub, combine all of the ingredients in a small bowl. When the ribs have finished soaking, take them out of the brine and pat them dry with paper towels. Rub a generous amount of the dry rub into the meaty areas.

Preheat the oven to 225°F (110°C). Wrap the ribs in aluminum foil, leaving a small opening on top so that air can circulate. Braise the ribs on the middle oven rack for 3 to 4 hours. After 2 hours, check the ribs at regular intervals to determine whether they're cooked all the way through. To do this, pierce the meat with a fork. The ribs are done when the juice that escapes is clear rather than pink. Be careful not to overcook them.

Preheat the grill to medium heat or 375°F (190°C), but don't let it get too hot. Position the grate one level higher than you normally would for steak so that the barbecue sauce doesn't immediately burn. Brush a lot of barbecue sauce onto the ribs and grill them for about 30 minutes, turning them every 3 to 10 minutes and making sure that the barbecue sauce caramelizes but doesn't burn. Brush on two or three coatings of sauce each time you turn the ribs. You know the ribs are done when you can easily pull the meat off the bone.

TONY'S MARISCOCO

What do you get after a genuine birthday celebration? That's right: a genuine hangover. Bar owner Tony Perez showed us his favorite hangover remedy: *mariscoco*. We volunteered as guinea pigs and can confirm that it really helps, tastes fantastic, and is super healthy. The combination seems unusual to foreigners, but it's worth giving it a chance. Try something new. Naturally, *mariscoco* tastes best if you prepare it in a country that has fresh coconuts.

SERVES 4

2 COCONUTS
8 OUNCES (250 G) MEDIUM SHRIMP, COOKED AND CHOPPED
1¾ CUPS (250 G) PEELED AND CHOPPED CUCUMBER
4 CUPS (1 LITER) CLAMATO JUICE (OR THIN TOMATO JUICE, BUT REAL CLAMATO IS BEST!)

¼ CUP (60 ML) WORCESTERSHIRE SAUCE
¼ CUP (60 ML) LIME JUICE
1 TABLESPOON RED PEPPER FLAKES
1 TEASPOON COARSE SEA SALT

Drill a hole in the two soft eyes of the coconuts and pour the coconut milk into a glass. Then open the coconuts and remove the flesh. We usually did this with a machete. If you don't happen to have one handy, try using a rock or a hammer: Beat around the circumference of the coconut until it breaks into two halves and then dice the coconut meat finely.

Combine the shrimp, cucumber, coconut milk, coconut meat, Clamato, Worcestershire sauce, lime juice, red pepper flakes, and salt in a large bowl and mix well.

Pour this drink into four very large glasses or coconut halves, add a long spoon to each glass, and give yourself and your friends a refreshing, light, unbelievably healthy treat!

LATIN MARKETS

As we traveled through Latin America, we visited a lot of bigger and smaller cities where our favorite pastime was wandering through markets. These markets might be entire neighborhoods filled with stands or large, multistory market halls with hundreds of stands and booths. They were packed full of everything imaginable, from fruits, vegetables, meat, and fish to toys, wrestling masks, and baseball bats. We probably could have bought smuggled organs or enriched uranium if we'd rooted around long enough. The butcher stands in these markets are very different from those in other countries. We found entire calves' and pigs' heads displayed on the counters. Tripe hung from hooks in the ceiling. Besides pork and beefsteaks, roasts, and chops, there were also fresh cow stomachs, tongues, and skinned lambs. For many foreigners, this could seem strange at first, but it indicates a better relationship with meat consumption. Why shouldn't our meat departments remind us that every steak once had a face? If you eat meat, you should be aware of where it comes from and use as much of the animal as possible—meaning, you should include animal parts in your diet that aren't as popular in your native home as they used to be. Tripe, for instance, is loaded with essential vitamins and minerals. When you look at the meat displayed in the markets, it doesn't exactly inspire confidence—it sits there all day long, unrefriger-

ated, and sees its share of flies. But because meat used in Latin American cuisine is always roasted or simmered for hours, we didn't let it bother us too much and bought meat anyway. We suffered from minor indigestion a few times but, thankfully, not very often.

So how can you tell if meat is edible? It's best to rely on your senses. How does the meat look—is its surface dry? That means it's been lying around too long and you shouldn't buy it. Does it have a strong odor? Then no question, keep your hands off! Is it lying in greasy meat juices? Stay away. We always picked up products before buying them so that we could examine them thoroughly. It's also a good idea to get to the market as early in the day as possible; you'll have a much better chance of finding refrigerated meat.

When it comes to buying fish, there's really no problem if you're by the ocean. All the markets up and down the Pacific coast offered fish of all types and sizes, all completely fresh. We often saw small fishing boats coming ashore after a long night on the water to sell the fish directly out of their nets. Freshness is essential, especially when you're preparing ceviche (page 176). But the absolute high point of all the markets was the wide variety of plump, ripe fruits. Huge, brightly colored mountains of mangoes, papayas, and pineapples were

piled next to fruits we'd never even seen before. Some were sweet, some sour, some soft, some hard—we tried them all because we wanted to experience every texture. There were days when all we ate was fruit.

A special feature of Mexican markets is the wide variety of chile peppers. They come in all shapes and colors, dried and smoked, whole, and as powder or paste. Each chile has its own particular uses that best match its flavor properties. They're a science in themselves!

HOMEMADE SURF WAX

No, you can't eat it, even though it smells deliciously coconutty. But you can wax your surfboard with it! This surf wax is 100 percent biodegradable and will guarantee the necessary grip during your next session.

MAKES 10½ OUNCES (300 GRAMS)

7 OUNCES (200 G) BEESWAX (FROM
A PHARMACY OR HEALTH FOOD STORE)
¼ CUP (50 G) COCONUT OIL
1¾ OUNCES (50 G) NATURAL RESIN
(FROM A HARDWARE STORE)
1 (14-OUNCE) EMPTY TIN CAN
2 SMALL EMPTY YOGURT CONTAINERS

Chop the beeswax into small pieces and combine it with the oil and resin in the tin can.

Fill a pot with 4 inches (10 cm) of water, bring it to a boil, and place the can in the center of the pot. The water should simmer gently but not get too hot or the wax might burn to the bottom of the can. Keep stirring with a spoon until all the ingredients in the can have melted.

When everything is liquefied, carefully remove the can from the water and let cool for about 10 minutes. Pour the surf wax mixture into the yogurt containers and let it cool and harden for several hours. Then you'll have your own surf wax! It will keep for 1 month at room temperature before it will begin to dry out.

PUERTO ESCONDIDO
– THE VEGGIE CHAPTER

After leaving Jalisco, Nayarit, Colima, Michoacán, and Guerrero behind us, we finally arrived in Oaxaca or, more specifically, at the world-famous surf spot Escondido. The waves are competition level and ridden by talented residents and top international surfers. Surfing is possible every day. For the surf guide for this location, see page 132.

We stayed at Osa Mariposa, an idyllic vegetarian-vegan hostel that a friend from San Pancho had recommended. Using this as our home base, we tried to straighten out our car documents to the point where we'd be able to drive it across Latin American borders: We needed to get new license plates, register our names, stuff like that—purely formalities, right? But no, the repair fiasco was just the beginning of our car troubles. Now things really started to go downhill.

Fortunately for us, we'd met Blondy at Osa Mariposa. He was a great guy, appropriately named—his curly hair was bleached blond—with a number of interesting tattoos. Blondy was "the man" when it came to any sort of organizing or finagling. If you had the money, he could probably find you an albino hammerhead shark to buy for a pet. He came with us to the local authorities and bargained with the friendly lady bureaucrat over our new license plates. In Mexico, car titles are handled a little differently. A car belongs to the person who has the original receipt. A car might be 30 years old and have had umpteen different owners, but without the original receipt, you can't do a thing with it. When a car changes hands, you're supposed to write that Mr. XY sold the car to Ms. YZ on the back of the receipt.

According to Mexican law, no one without a permanent Mexican residence can register a car in their name, so our plan was to officially register the car under Blondy's name and then get a notarized use permit for the rest of our trip. But according to the lady behind the counter, the registration process would take about six weeks! Things were looking bad. Blondy called up another official and asked whether we could get the license plates just a little bit faster and—wham! Now we were really up shit creek. The guy made an interesting discovery when he looked up our license number: Our car had been reported stolen. Fuck. We looked at the documents more closely and noticed that someone had altered them with Wite-Out and a copy machine. Okay, now what? We had to ditch the car, but without the proper documents…? When we mentioned this to Blondy, he just grinned and told us it was about time we let go of our European obsession with right and wrong. Mexico was full of people who were willing to buy a car without documentation.

Whatever the outcome of this shady transaction, one thing was clear: Our departure would be postponed. Frustrated, we decided to at least take advantage of the opportunity to get some more tattoos. Jo scribbled down a few ideas on a piece of paper, which we then took to a local tattoo shop and had transferred to our bodies: a tiny ship, for each of us. Jo also got a cactus above his ankle and half a lemon on his wrist. Cozy treated himself to a fleeing bank robber on his shoulder blade. Then we went and had a beer.

A week later, after being initiated in the car-fencing business, we started working as chefs at Osa Mariposa in exchange for our room and board. We were able to teach our boss, Jade, a lot about vegetarian and vegan cooking—food that, I'm ashamed to say, hadn't been a large part of our diet up to that point. We field-tested our creations every evening at Osa Mariposa's family-style dinners, when guests and employees all sat around one long table and celebrated the day's end. It was incredibly hard to whip up creative vegan and vegetarian dishes for 20 to 30 people day after day, especially on a total budget of around 18 euros. Fortunately, vegetables in Mexico were dirt-cheap, so we spent most of our daily allowance at the market and used the little remaining money to buy something special to spruce up the menu, like walnuts, dried fruits, or maybe a special spice. Some ingredients, such as coconuts, we could take from the neighbor's palm tree. Mangoes were also in season, and the tree in the garden gave us pound after pound of ripe, juicy mangoes every day.

GRILLED VEGETABLE TERIYAKI SALAD

WITH CILANTRO SAUCE AND WALNUTS

SERVES 5

1 POUND (500 G) NEW POTATOES, PEELED

2 STALKS CELERY, CHOPPED

1 ZUCCHINI, DICED

2 CARROTS, PEELED AND DICED

1 CUP (100 G) GREEN BEANS

2¾ CUPS (100 G) SWISS CHARD, RIBS REMOVED

1 LARGE BEET, PEELED AND CHOPPED

1 TABLESPOON OLIVE OIL

1 SMALL RED ONION, SLICED INTO RINGS

2¾ CUPS (100 G) DAY-OLD WHITE BREAD, DICED

½ CUP (50 G) BUTTON MUSHROOMS, CHOPPED

1 RED BELL PEPPER, SEEDED AND DICED

1 SMALL EGGPLANT, CHOPPED

2 PEACHES, SLICED INTO WEDGES

HANDFUL OF SPINACH

1 TABLESPOON TERIYAKI SAUCE

CILANTRO SALSA (PAGE 53)

NICA SAUCE (PAGE 52)

HANDFUL OF WALNUTS, CHOPPED

½ BUNCH CILANTRO, CHOPPED

Bring a pot of water to a boil. Boil the potatoes in the water for about 20 minutes, or until a knife inserted goes into the flesh of a potato without any effort. Remove the potatoes from the water, drain, and place in a large salad bowl.

Bring a second pot of water to a boil and blanch the celery pieces for about 3 minutes. Remove the celery using a slotted spoon and place in ice water for 20 seconds. Then drain and transfer the celery to the salad bowl. Blanch the zucchini, carrots, beans, and chard for 2 minutes each, and the beet for 3 minutes. The beet will turn the water red so it's best to do it last. Transfer the vegetables to the salad bowl as they are cooked and drained.

Heat the olive oil in a skillet over medium-high heat and sauté the onion rings for about 10 minutes, or until they're translucent and golden brown around the edges. Place them in the salad bowl.

Using the same pan, sauté the bread cubes and the mushrooms, bell peppers, and eggplant one by one for 2 to 3 minutes each, until all the cubes are crisp and brown around the edges. Layer these ingredients in the salad bowl. Although it takes longer to sauté the vegetables one at a time, it works better than mixing them all together in the pan.

Finally, add the peaches and spinach to the bowl. Drizzle the salad with a little teriyaki sauce and toss it gently.

Divide the salad among serving plates and top each serving with 1 tablespoon cilantro sauce and 1 tablespoon nica sauce. Sprinkle it with walnuts and cilantro leaves. Your salad is ready to serve.

TROPICAL CURRY

SERVES 5

BASIC CURRY SAUCE

CURRY PASTE (PAGE 143)

4 CUPS (1 LITER)
VEGETABLE STOCK

1³/₄ CUPS (420 ML) COCONUT MILK

1¹/₃ CUPS (250 G) WHITE RICE

MIXED VEGETABLES

VEGETABLE OIL, FOR FRYING

1 LARGE RED ONION, SLICED INTO 8 WEDGES

1 PINEAPPLE, PEELED AND DICED

1 BANANA, PEELED AND SLICED

1 POUND (500 G) NEW POTATOES, PEELED
AND HALVED

2 CARROTS, PEELED, HALVED, AND SLICED

1 RED BELL PEPPER, SEEDED AND DICED

1 BUNCH MINT, CHOPPED

1 BUNCH CILANTRO, CHOPPED

2 STALKS LEMONGRASS, CHOPPED

2 TABLESPOONS PUMPKIN SEEDS

5 (8 BY 12-INCH/20 BY 30 CM) BANANA
LEAVES, RINSED

To make the curry sauce, toast the curry paste in a pot over medium heat until golden brown. Then add the vegetable stock and coconut milk. Stir the mixture well, cover, and simmer for 30 minutes.

In the meantime, place the rice and 2¾ cups (660 ml) water in a second pot and bring it to a boil. Cover the pot and simmer the rice over medium heat for 20 minutes.

To prepare the vegetables, heat a little vegetable oil in a skillet over medium heat and sauté the onion for about 10 minutes, or until translucent. Then turn up the heat and sauté for another 2 minutes, or until crisp and brown. Transfer the onion to a large bowl and set aside.

Briefly sauté the pineapple and the banana with a little more oil in the pan for 5 to 8 minutes, then add the potatoes, carrots, and peppers and sauté over high heat for another 5 to 8 minutes. As soon as the pieces turn golden brown around the edges, they're perfectly done. When done, add them to the bowl with the onion.

Add the mint, cilantro, lemongrass, pumpkin seeds, and curry sauce to the bowl of sautéed vegetables and fruit and stir carefully.

Lay out the banana leaves and place a serving of rice on top of each. Fill each leaf with lots of curry—but make sure they can still be folded! Then fold three sides in toward the center and secure them with a toothpick. Done!

DAVE'S BLACK BEAN BURGERS

Dave, the founder of Osa Mariposa, gave us this recipe for his awesome vegan bean burger. Okay, there's no "quick & easy" version of this recipe, but it's definitely worth the trouble. And as long as you're at it, we recommend that you make a little extra filling and freeze it—for a planned dinner, or for when friends drop by unexpectedly...or just for yourself!

SERVES 6

PATTIES

5 CUPS (850 G) COOKED BLACK BEANS

3/4 CUP (80 G) BREAD CRUMBS

1/3 CUP (45 G) QUICK-COOKING ROLLED OATS

2 TABLESPOONS (30 G) KETCHUP

1 MEDIUM CARROT, GRATED

1 TEASPOON VEGETABLE OIL, PLUS MORE FOR FRYING

1/2 MEDIUM RED ONION, FINELY CHOPPED

1/2 MEDIUM ZUCCHINI, FINELY CHOPPED

2 CLOVES GARLIC, MINCED

1 JALAPEÑO CHILE, SEEDED AND MINCED

1 3/4 CUPS (30 G) FRESH CILANTRO LEAVES

1/2 TEASPOON GROUND CUMIN

1/2 TEASPOON DRIED OREGANO

1/2 TEASPOON CHILI POWDER

2 TABLESPOONS (30 ML) OLIVE OIL

1/2 TEASPOON SALT

1/2 TEASPOON FRESHLY GROUND BLACK PEPPER

1 CUP (250 G) POPPED AMARANTH

PLUS

HANDFUL OF BABY GREEN ASPARAGUS

3 TABLESPOONS OLIVE OIL

1 SMALL RED ONION, SLICED INTO RINGS

1/4 RED CABBAGE, SLICED INTO STRIPS

2 TABLESPOONS APPLE CIDER VINEGAR

1 AVOCADO, PITTED, PEELED, AND SLICED

1 TOMATO, SLICED

6 HAMBURGER BUNS

CHIPOTLE-LIME SAUCE (PAGE 51)

In a large bowl, mash the black beans until smooth using a potato masher. It's okay if some of the beans are still whole. Add the bread crumbs, oats, ketchup, and carrot to the mashed beans and mix together thoroughly. Don't be afraid to get your hands dirty!

Heat the vegetable oil in a skillet and braise the onions and zucchini for 5 minutes, stirring occasionally, until they're tender and golden brown. Add the onions and zucchini to the bean mixture.

Purée the garlic, jalapeño, cilantro, cumin, oregano, chili powder, and olive oil in a blender to make a creamy paste. Add this paste to the bean mixture, mix it thoroughly, and season it with the salt and pepper.

Sprinkle a little amaranth onto a large, flat plate and place another empty plate beside it. Shape the bean mixture into 12 balls the size of golf balls and flatten them into patties. Dredge both sides in the amaranth until they're completely covered. Place the finished patties on the empty plate.

Your burger patties are now ready for frying or freezing! If you want to store the patties in a stack, place a small piece of parchment paper between them so they won't stick together. You can keep them in the refrigerator for up to 1 week or freeze them for up to 2 months.

If you're cooking them immediately: In a pan, fry the patties in a little vegetable oil over medium heat for 3 minutes on each side, or until they're nice and brown. Place them on a plate covered with plastic wrap after they are done cooking to keep them warm while you finish cooking all of the patties. If you're taking them directly from the freezer, allow 5 minutes on each side. You can cover the frying pan with a lid or another pan to ensure that the burgers cook evenly, inside and out.

While the patties are frying, prepare the garnishes. Sauté the asparagus in a small pan in 1 tablespoon of the olive oil until it develops rusty brown spots. Season with salt and set aside.

Sauté the onion rings in 1 tablespoon of the olive oil until it looks nicely toasted. Set aside.

Sauté the cabbage in the remaining 1 tablespoon olive oil until soft, and then add the vinegar. Remove the pan from the heat and let the cabbage stand briefly while you assemble the burgers.

Now it's assembly time! Serve each burger on a hamburger bun with 2 patties, avocado, tomato, vegetables, and chipotle-lime sauce. Enjoy!

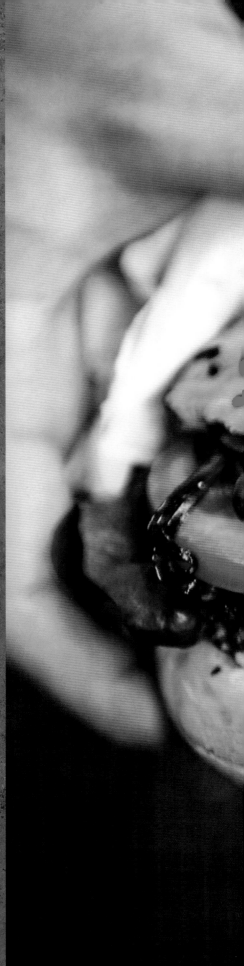

VEGGIE

MEXICAN RAVIOLI
WITH TWO TYPES OF FILLING

SERVES 4

RAVIOLI
3⅓ CUPS (500 G) TYPE "00" FLOUR
5 MEDIUM EGGS
2 TABLESPOONS OLIVE OIL, PLUS MORE FOR COOKING
1 TEASPOON SALT, PLUS MORE FOR COOKING
ALL-PURPOSE FLOUR, FOR THE WORK SURFACE

FILLINGS (SEE PAGE 131)
SAGE BUTTER OR TOMATO SAUCE, FOR SERVING

Knead the flour, eggs, oil, and salt together in a large bowl for about 10 to 12 minutes, or until you have a smooth, pliable dough. Cover the dough and let stand in a cool place for 1 hour so it won't shrink when you roll it out later on.

Dust a large, smooth work surface with a little flour and roll out the dough in batches to a thickness of 1/16 inch (2 mm) using a rolling pin or a pasta maker. It's a little harder with a rolling pin, but it works and it's worth it! Cut the dough into long strips and then into equal-size squares of about 3 inches (8 cm).

Place a small mound of filling on half the squares and moisten the edges with a little water. Place the other squares on top and press them securely together around the edges with the tines of a fork. This takes a little practice but it's really no big deal. Let your fresh ravioli dry for about 1 hour.

Bring a large pot of water to a boil with a little salt and 2 tablespoons oil. Add the ravioli and cook them for 2 minutes. After boiling, we like to sauté our ravioli in sage butter, but you can also serve them with tomato sauce, depending on your preference.

SPICY MANGO-RICOTTA FILLING

1 MANGO, PEELED, PITTED, AND FINELY DICED

2/3 CUP (150 G) RICOTTA CHEESE

HANDFUL OF FRESH MINT, CHOPPED

1 TEASPOON RED PEPPER FLAKES

1/2 TEASPOON SALT

Mix together the mango and ricotta to make a paste. Fold in the mint and red pepper flakes and season the mixture with the salt.

CILANTRO-BEAN FILLING

2/3 CUP (100 G) COOKED BLACK BEANS

2 HANDFULS FRESH CILANTRO, MINCED

JUICE OF 1 LIME

1 CLOVE GARLIC, PEELED

SALT AND FRESHLY GROUND BLACK PEPPER

Mash the cooked beans into a smooth pulp using a potato masher. Add the cilantro and lime juice to the bean mixture. Squeeze the garlic through a press and add. Stir everything together with a spoon and season it with salt and pepper.

MEXICO SURF GUIDE // PART IV
PUERTO ESCONDIDO

We surfed three world-class spots in Puerto Escondido:

ZICATELA 15.85365°N −97.05775°E

This is by far the most famous spot in Puerto Escondido. Like Pascuales (page 102), the swell from the open sea hits the flat sandbanks so freely and relentlessly that you can find real monster waves. The waves are at least 20 feet (6 meters) high and break in enormous, hollow, extremely powerful barrels. Despite the wave height, the water is extremely shallow, so broken boards and broken bones are fairly common. This is where the big-wave elite come to surf. Anyone who rides the main peak had better be damn sure they know what they're doing. After just a few minutes, Jo's board broke on a wave that was less than 6½ feet (2 meters) high.

PUNTA ZICATELA 15.83000°N −97.04819°E

This left point break is at the south end of the main beach. The waves here aren't as deadly as those at Zicatela, but that means it's much more crowded. No matter how early you start, there's always someone there ahead of you. Watch out for the rocks near the beach—there are a few of them lurking just below the surface! On good days, the waves can be surfed for over 330 feet (100 meters), including barrel sections.

COLOTEPEC 15.80629°N -97.01871°E

This killer spot is about a five-minute drive from Puerto Escondido at a river mouth. Due to sediment from the river, the water is kind of brown and muddy, and a crocodile or two could be lying in wait—if you believe the locals' stories. The finest barrels break over sand, both to the left and to the right of the river. But be careful, as entrances and exits can get a little complicated when there's a decent swell.

After five tough weeks, we finally found a shifty enough buyer for our car. He met us on a deserted beach access road under a bridge and handed over a bag of small bills for the car. That was probably the closest we'll ever come to a gangster movie experience. We were mad at ourselves for being so naive about car buying but extremely happy to finally be out of the whole mess and booking a flight to Managua, Nicaragua. Because we'd spent so much time in Cuba and Mexico, we unfortunately had to skip Guatemala, El Salvador, and Honduras. But it was definitely time to go. After almost three fantastic months in Mexico, we'd drunk enough tequila to last a lifetime.

ARAGUA

SEE VIDEO:

Nicaragua is one of the poorest countries in Central America, which is obvious when you see the products available and, of course, the people's housing conditions.

In small villages especially, many of the tiny shacks are without electricity or running water. What Nicaragua does have, however, is fantastic waves. The entire coastline is one awesome surf spot after another. Nicaragua isn't yet overrun with tourists because many people still associate it with the war between the CIA and drug cartels in the 1980s. Incidentally, we never felt unsafe or unwelcome at any time, anywhere in Nicaragua. It probably won't take long for the crowds to find their way there, but meanwhile—if you like volcanoes, jungles, waves, and fresh fish, there's no better place to be!

Cerro Negro

LEÓN

MANAGUA

GRANADA

Playa
Chacocente

Lance's Left

Popoyo

Playa Santana

Playa Colorado

SAN JUAN
DEL SUR

Playa
Amarilla

I n Nicaragua we mainly got around in "chicken buses." After enjoying a long, useful life in the United States, these old yellow school buses were sold to Nicaragua. Now they rattle around the countryside, indestructible, even over dirt roads and to the most remote villages. One of these buses took us to Masachapa and Pochomil, two fishing villages practically merged into one on about the same latitude as Managua, the Nicaraguan capital. Pochomil has a nice beach break that's mainly suitable for beginners. The waves aren't generally as high or as fast as in the better-known spots farther south. It's a place to relax and do nothing because—other than hanging around in a hammock or on the beach—there is in fact nothing to do. One exception is a little event that takes place on the beach at Masachapa every morning at sunrise and is definitely worth seeing: the fishermen

returning with their nightly catch. The fish are weighed and sold right from the boats: tuna, snapper, mackerel, and skate galore, so fresh that they smell only of seawater. One of the boats we saw had only four fish on board: bull sharks, each about 6½ feet (2 meters) long. What must they taste like? We started out with a breakfast of tortillas and fresh grilled fish from a shack at the harbor and watched the women doing business while the exhausted fishermen lounged around among huge piles of fishing nets and ropes, drinking cups of hot coffee and recovering from a night of backbreaking work. Then we tried to do some business with the Nicaraguan women ourselves. It was brutal. After a series of hard-core negotiations, we finally came away with a magnificent 5-pound (2.2 kg) snapper and felt lucky not to have been talked into marrying a fisherman's daughter or renovating someone's house.

FAST FOOD

YELLOW FISH CURRY

1 BUNCH BROCCOLI
3 TABLESPOONS CURRY PASTE
(RECIPE FOLLOWS, OR STORE-BOUGHT)
1¾ CUPS (420 ML) COCONUT MILK
4 CUPS (1 LITER) HEARTY VEGETABLE STOCK
4 TOMATOES, SLICED INTO EIGHTHS
2¾ CUPS (300 G) SNOW PEAS
3 TABLESPOONS OLIVE OIL
2¼ POUNDS (1 KG) FIRM FISH FILLETS
(SUCH AS SNAPPER, COD, HALIBUT, OR TUNA),
CUT INTO BITE-SIZE PIECES

2 SCALLIONS, THINLY SLICED
1 CHILE PEPPER, SEEDED AND MINCED
½ BUNCH CILANTRO, MINCED
BLACK SESAME SEEDS, FOR GARNISH

CURRY PASTE

2 TABLESPOONS CORIANDER SEEDS
1 TABLESPOON FENNEL SEEDS
1 CINNAMON STICK
2 TABLESPOONS GROUND TURMERIC
1 TABLESPOON SALT
1 TABLESPOON GROUND CUMIN
1 TEASPOON GROUND NUTMEG
10 DRIED CHILE PEPPERS
10 CLOVES GARLIC (YEAH, MANI)
5 SHALLOTS
3 STALKS LEMONGRASS
1 INCH (2½ CM) FRESH GINGER (EVEN
BETTER, GALANGAL!)
¼ CUP (60 ML) TOASTED SESAME OIL

143

Divide the broccoli into florets and cut them into bite-size pieces. Sear the curry paste in a large wok over medium-high heat for 2 minutes to bring out its full flavor. Add the coconut milk and stock and reduce slightly over medium heat for 15 minutes.

Add the broccoli, tomatoes, and snow peas to the curry stock and stir it well. Simmer the curry for 5 minutes.

Heat the oil in a skillet over medium heat and cook the fish for 5 to 7 minutes per side. Distribute the curry in serving bowls. Add the fish, top with scallions, chile pepper, cilantro, and black sesame seeds, and enjoy!

Toast the coriander seeds, fennel seeds, and cinnamon stick in a dry skillet over medium heat for several minutes, or until they develop a nice fragrance. Place these spices and all of the remaining ingredients in a blender or food processor and purée to make a creamy paste. Take a good whiff. Any questions? You can store this in the refrigerator for up to 2 weeks, but I bet you'll use it faster than it will spoil!

AT THE NICA MARKET

The markets in Managua, the capital of Nicaragua, are actually small villages under corrugated iron roofs. Early in the morning, we brought our growling stomachs to one of these markets, called Roberto Huembes, on Boulevard Don Bosco. We stood at a niche that we were told was the entrance. What looked inconspicuous and peaceful from the outside was like an ant farm inside. It seemed like all hell had broken loose, even at seven in the morning. After walking just 6½ feet (or about 2 meters) into the iron maze, we found ourselves in a small food hall. Everywhere we looked, there were gigantic metal cauldrons perched over hot coals, filled with soups of every description. Here and there, an incredibly wrinkled granny would dig down into a bubbling pot and bring up a ladleful of amazing things from the very depths: whole bright red crabs, half a veal shank—in one pot we even saw cows' eyes. Single rays of sunlight filtered through the jury-rigged, corrugated roof and filled the entire scene with a dim glow. It was a little like standing in a witch's kitchen—but with friendly witches.

When we asked the old women about their concoctions, their faces lit up. They were happy to share their culinary secrets with us and let us taste anything we wanted. Their soups tasted exactly the way they looked—unbelievably delicious.

NICARAGUAN MARKET SOUP

SERVES 4

2½ CUPS (450 G) CANNED WHITE BEANS, RINSED
AND DRAINED
1 TOMATO, SLICED INTO EIGHTHS
1 GREEN BELL PEPPER, SEEDED AND DICED
1 MEDIUM YELLOW ONION, FINELY CHOPPED
4 CLOVES GARLIC, MINCED
¼ CUP (70 G) TOMATO PASTE
1 POUND (500 G) BEEF BONES
5 BAY LEAVES
4 PORK SHOULDER CHOPS, CUT INTO ¾-INCH (2 CM) CUBES
5 RUSSET POTATOES, COOKED, PEELED, AND DICED
5 TABLESPOONS WORCESTERSHIRE SAUCE
JUICE OF 1 LIME, PLUS MORE FOR SERVING
2 TABLESPOONS YELLOW MUSTARD
3 TABLESPOONS LIGHT BROWN SUGAR
SALT AND FRESHLY GROUND BLACK PEPPER
3¾ OUNCES (110 G) PARMESAN
CHOPPED FRESH PARSLEY AND RED PEPPER FLAKES,
FOR SERVING

Add three-quarters of the beans plus the tomatoes, bell pepper, onion, garlic, tomato paste, soup bones, and bay leaves to a pot containing 8 cups (2 liters) water and bring to a boil. Cover the pot and simmer the soup over medium heat for 15 minutes. Decrease the heat and add the pork. Cover and simmer the soup over low heat for 1 hour, or until the pork is nice and tender.

Purée the remaining one-quarter of the beans with 2 handfuls of diced potatoes. Add this and the rest of the diced potatoes to the soup. Stir well and add the Worcestershire sauce, lime juice, mustard, sugar, and salt and pepper to taste. Grate the Parmesan over the top. Let the soup stand for another 10 minutes, until the Parmesan has made it nice and creamy. Transfer the soup to serving bowls and top with a little lime juice, parsley, and chili flakes—and it's done!

NACATAMALES

As we wandered through the market, we discovered loads of new items in every corner: super-spicy chicken wings sizzling over an open fire, an old man selling grilled corn on the cob. We were especially drawn to the *nacatamales*, small packets consisting of a banana leaf wrapped around a rice mixture and buttery, juicy meat. Serve one or two of these per person, depending on how hungry you are.

MAKES 6 TAMALES

CORN FILLING

1 TOMATO, DICED

1 FRESH GREEN CHILE PEPPER, SEEDED AND MINCED

½ MEDIUM YELLOW ONION, DICED

1 CLOVE GARLIC, MINCED

1¾ CUPS (300 G) YELLOW CORNMEAL

JUICE OF ½ ORANGE

JUICE OF 2 LIMES

2 TABLESPOONS APPLE CIDER VINEGAR

½ CUP (100 G) LARD

15 MINT LEAVES

1 TABLESPOON SEA SALT

MEAT FILLING

1 TEASPOON GROUND CUMIN

1 TEASPOON CHILI POWDER

1 TEASPOON DRIED OREGANO

1 TEASPOON GARLIC POWDER

1 TEASPOON GROUND TURMERIC

1 TEASPOON SEA SALT

1 TEASPOON FRESHLY GROUND BLACK PEPPER

2¼ POUNDS (1 KG) PORK ROAST, CUT INTO 1-INCH (3 CM) CUBES

RICE FILLING

2 MEDIUM POTATOES, PEELED AND DICED

1 RED BELL PEPPER, SEEDED AND DICED

1 MEDIUM YELLOW ONION, DICED

1 BUNCH MINT, TORN INTO PIECES

¾ CUP (150 G) WHITE RICE, SOAKED IN WARM WATER FOR AT LEAST 30 MINUTES

HANDFUL OF RAISINS

2 TABLESPOONS LIME JUICE, PLUS MORE FOR DRIZZLING

PACKETS

6 BANANA LEAVES, CUT INTO 10-INCH (25 CM) SQUARES (OR PARCHMENT PAPER)

Cut away the central stems of the banana leaves so you can use them later to tie up the tamales. Kitchen string will also work

To make the corn filling, mix together all of the ingredients in a large bowl with 1½ cups (360 ml) water. Purée this mixture in a blender until fairly smooth. (It should have the consistency of firm mashed potatoes.) Let the mixture stand for at least 30 minutes.

To make the meat filling, mix all of the spices in a shallow bowl and dredge the meat cubes in the spices. Cover the meat and let it stand in a cool place for 1 hour.

To make the rice filling, combine all of the ingredients in a bowl.

Cut six sheets of aluminum foil to the same size as your banana leaves. Spread out a banana leaf with the soft inner side up. Put 2 to 3 tablespoons of the corn mixture in the middle and spread it around with a spoon. Place several pork cubes and a little of the rice filling in the center and drizzle lime juice over everything.

Fold one side of the leaf toward the center, against the grain, then fold in the side across from it, and finally the other two sides. (Simply put: Fold it into a packet.) Tie up the packet with the strong central stem from the banana leaf (or with kitchen string). Turn the packet over so that the smooth side is on top. Place the filled packet in the middle of a sheet of aluminum foil. Fold up the foil the same way you did the banana leaf. Repeat with the remaining 5 banana leaves.

Fill a large vegetable steamer with 2 inches (5 cm) of water and bring it to a boil. Decrease the heat under the steamer and place the prepared packets in the steamer insert. Steam the *nacatamales* over low heat for at least 2 hours—or even better, for 3 hours—checking occasionally to make sure there's still water in the pot and adding more as necessary.

Remove the steamed packets from the pot and let them cool for 15 minutes. Unwrap the banana leaves, and the filling is now ready to eat. (Discard and do not consume the banana leaves after you have enjoyed the filling.)

In addition to the *nacatamales*, we found a small stand offering freshly squeezed juices. At the same time, the irresistible aroma of pitch-black coffee—typical of Nicaragua and probably strong enough to wake the dead—wafted over the market. After we'd stuffed ourselves with every kind of treat imaginable, curiosity pulled us deeper into the maze. There seemed to be no logical order. A stand selling piñatas and dolls in every possible shade of pink stood next to a mustachioed fruit peddler. Nearby were a stand selling used cell phones, a shoe vendor, and—for a change—a vegetable woman. After turning many more corners in the maze and diving deep into the throng, we finally reached the heart of the market: an enormous hall with countless individual stands selling different types of meat and fish. The dull thump of meat cleavers on tree stumps was combined with the loud yammering of vendors peddling their wares. In one corner, a little boy was feeding three parrots that just stood on the open cage door. The reason they didn't try to fly away was probably because they knew they'd never find their way out through the total chaos—same as us.

There were also unusual foods that would take more getting used to: Some vendors were selling bright green iguanas, bound by their legs. Not as pets—these lizards were headed for the pot. I gagged a little as I remembered our overnight bus trip to Nicaragua. I'd bought a banana leaf wrapped around cornmeal and some kind of mystery meat from one of the locals who'd jumped on the bus to sell snacks. When I asked him what I was eating, he proudly explained that it was the finest iguana. It didn't bother me at the time; it tasted good. But now...looking into the tired eyes of the bound iguana, I knew I could never eat it again. We hurried on by, snaking our way along the narrow market paths until we finally managed to get near an exit. As the crowd gradually thinned out, we finally found ourselves outside again, where women in booths were laughing and joking as they shaped cornmeal into little tortillas with skillful hand movements. They let us have a try, too, but it wasn't as easy as it looked. The cornmeal constantly stuck to our fingers, and our tortillas looked more like deformed pizza crusts, to the women's great amusement.

Next door there were huge metal cauldrons filled with crisp slices of spicy blood sausage and polenta chips. People were lining up to get their share. We figured there must be a reason, so we got in line along with them. And once again, it was totally awesome. The spicy, earthy notes of the blood sausage were perfectly balanced by the tart, pickled cabbage salad, while the mild, sweet flavor of the golden brown polenta chips pulled it all together. The people at the market really knew their stuff—there's no other way to explain it.

FLAMBÉED BLOOD SAUSAGE

WITH CABBAGE SALAD AND POLENTA CHIPS

SERVES 4

CABBAGE SALAD (CURTIDO)

1 SMALL HEAD WHITE CABBAGE, GRATED

2 CARROTS, GRATED

1 SMALL RED ONION, THINLY SLICED

1 RED BELL PEPPER, SEEDED AND SLICED INTO STRIPS

¼ CUP RAISINS

1 CUP (240 ML) APPLE CIDER VINEGAR

¼ CUP GINGER SYRUP (PAGE 178)

1 TABLESPOON DRIED OREGANO

1 TABLESPOON SALT

1 TEASPOON FINELY GROUND DRIED CHILE PEPPERS

POLENTA

2 CUPS (480 ML) MILK

1¾ CUPS (420 ML) VEGETABLE STOCK

1½ CUPS (250 G) POLENTA

1¾ OUNCES (50 G) FIRM GOAT CHEESE, DICED

1 TABLESPOON GROUND TURMERIC

1 TEASPOON SALT

VEGETABLE OIL, FOR FRYING

BLOOD SAUSAGES

1¾ POUNDS (800 G) HIGH-QUALITY BLOOD SAUSAGE (FROM A BUTCHER)

VEGETABLE OIL, FOR FRYING

⅓ CUP (80 ML) RUM (WE LIKE FLOR DE CAÑA 7-YEAR-OLD)

1 TABLESPOON HONEY

SALT AND FRESHLY GROUND BLACK PEPPER

To make the cabbage salad, in a large bowl, combine all of the ingredients with 3¾ cups (900 ml) water, mix thoroughly, and transfer to a large canning jar. Refrigerate the salad for at least 24 hours. In a sealed, airtight jar, it will keep for up to 4 weeks!

To make the polenta, in a heavy pot, bring the milk and vegetable stock to a simmer. Decrease the heat and gradually add the polenta, stirring all the while to prevent lumps. Cover the pot and simmer for 10 minutes.

Stir the cheese, turmeric, and salt into the polenta. Remove the pot from the heat and let the polenta stand for 15 minutes. Then spread it out evenly on a baking sheet and let it cool. The polenta will become relatively firm.

Fill a deep pot with a few inches of oil and heat over medium-high heat. Cut the polenta into diamond-shaped pieces and deep-fry them for 1 to 2 minutes, then drain on paper towels.

To prepare the sausage, slice the blood sausage on an angle. Heat a little oil to a very high temperature in a large pan and sear the blood sausage for 2 to 3 minutes, while stirring. Pour in the rum and carefully light it with a lighter. Let the rum burn off while swirling the pan or stirring. When the flame dies out, lower the heat, drizzle the sausage with honey, and sizzle it for a few more minutes, stirring it occasionally. Finally, season it with salt and pepper. If the blood sausage is too greasy, drain it briefly on a plate lined with paper towels.

Spread out the cabbage salad in a 6 x 9-inch (15 by 23 cm) casserole dish. Arrange the blood sausage and fried polenta chips and serve immediately. This dish goes well with Port or a hearty red wine.

SLOW FOOD

VIGORÓN

As we traveled farther south, we passed through Granada, a beautiful, colonial-style city. It was at a market there that we had our first encounter with *vigorón*, one of our favorite Nicaraguan dishes and typical of the Granada region. It's sold very cheaply at many markets.

Vigorón is made of cooked cassava, crisp pork, and *curtido*, a salad comprised of cabbage, onions, tomatoes, carrots, and sometimes lime juice. (This is the salad we made with our blood sausage dish on page 152). To be authentic, it should stand for an hour so that it can ferment slightly. It's then topped with a dressing containing small pickled chile peppers. It's typically served in a banana leaf and eaten with your fingers—which is how we always prefer to eat, anyway.

155

SERVES 4

- 12 CUPS (3 LITERS) VEGETABLE STOCK, PLUS MORE IF NEEDED
- 3⅔ CUPS (750 G) CASSAVA, PEELED
- 2¼ POUNDS (1 KG) PORK BELLY
- VEGETABLE OIL, FOR FRYING
- 4 PLATE-SIZE PIECES OF BANANA LEAF
- 7 CUPS (500 G) CABBAGE SALAD (PAGE 152)
- 1 TABLESPOON CARAWAY SEEDS
- ALIÑO CRIOLLO (PAGE 52)

Bring a large pot with the vegetable stock to a boil. Add the cassava and pork belly and boil for about 1 hour. There should always be enough stock in the pot to cover the pork. (If 3 liters aren't enough, add a little more.)

Remove the cassava from the stock using a slotted spoon, let it cool briefly, and cut it into bite-size pieces. Cut the pork belly into bite-size pieces.

Heat a few inches of vegetable oil in a deep pot and deep-fry the pork pieces for 3 minutes. Because the meat was precooked, it will stay tender on the inside while the fatty rind will become extremely crisp.

Spread out the banana leaves on a board or plates, place a small mound of cabbage salad in the center of each, and top it with the deep-fried pork and cassava. Season with the caraway and chili sauce. Dig in! This typically contains Bavarian cabbage salad, but you don't have to be Bavarian to love it!

OLD FRIENDS

We took a bus to Jiquelite to meet up with some old friends from Australia who happened to be on a surf trip in Nicaragua at the same time as us. But unlike us, they were there for a few weeks of vacation, so they'd booked an all-inclusive surf trip package at the Buena Onda Beach Resort. Seven friends were occupying two comfortable houses with lots of hammocks and unlimited beer. The package included two surf guides, who chauffeured them to the best spots in the area in giant 4-by-4 jeeps. Meanwhile, we rented a small, dilapidated back room at a nearby restaurant. When the surf guides realized that we had a 200-500 mm lens on our camera, they made us an unexpected offer. The photographer that the Australians had booked as part of their overall package hadn't shown up. A lucky break for us, and an offer we couldn't possibly refuse: $500 in cash and a ride to the spots where we'd take the photos. Brilliant! We took turns—one of us surfing while the other took pictures. And to top it all off, we were allowed to help ourselves to the group's beer and chocolate supplies. This allowed us to surf the best spots in Nicaragua with our friends, including some spots we never would have found on our own. Life is good!

NICARAGUA SURF GUIDE

Nicaragua has a fundamental surfing advantage: The enormous Lago Nicaragua acts as a giant wind machine that sends offshore winds to the coast practically year-round. This means perfectly formed waves—in fact, some of the best waves of our entire trip. The photos are worth a thousand words.

PLAYA COLORADO 11.40573°N -86.04952°E

Beach break, barrel paradise. Has the most famous waves, so it's always crowded.

PLAYA CHACOCENTE 11.53744°N -86.19545°E

Tip: This spot is in the middle of a turtle reserve guarded by soldiers. On days when turtles have been sighted in the water, surfing is prohibited. It's worth taking a look, though it can only be reached in a 4-by-4 jeep.

PLAYA SANTANA 11.45902°N -86.11131°E

Beach break/shore break. This spot has three peaks, the one on the far left generally being the highest. Lots of locals but an overall friendly atmosphere.

SANTANA

CHACOCENTE

PLAYA AMARILLA 11.39553"N -86.03581"E

Beach break, good for beginners. A little more protected than its "big brother" Colorado, one bay over.

POPOYO 11.45902"N -86.11131"E

Consistent A-frames, a well-known spot that attracts lots of people. In a small surf bar on a hillside nearby, we enjoyed a cold beer and a perfect view of the surf.

LANCE'S LEFT 11.52332°N -86.17714°E

Left-hand point break, accessible by boat or on foot from Astillero.

As our farewell to Nicaragua, we participated in the famous "Sunny Funday" in San Juan del Sur, a party thrown by three large hostels located on the surrounding hills. All three hostels had large pools and a shuttle service between them. The party had already started at around noon, with techno music that was loud but good. The whole thing slowly escalated throughout the afternoon, and by sunset, it was no-holds-barred. We can't possibly describe the magnitude of this binge because we can't remember any of it—and it's probably better that way.

Costa
Rica...

SEE VIDEO:

TAMARINDO

PLAYA SANTA TERESA

Montezuma

People call Costa Rica the Switzerland of Latin America, and when you see how much a piece of cheese costs, you understand why. But when you taste the cheese, the comparison quickly falls apart. It's expensive but flavorless. Cooking good and balanced meals wasn't so easy there because we couldn't afford to pay $10 for a supermarket steak. Apart from the prices, however, the country is insanely beautiful. Whales breach along the coast, monkeys greet you in hostel gardens, and the water is bathtub temperature.

If you look around a little, you can find a quiet little spot all to yourself in largely wide-open Costa Rica. On the Nicoya Peninsula there are several hard-to-reach beaches filled with endless quiet. The jungle often reaches right up to the ocean, and you feel cut off from the world. You can pick bananas and coconuts right from the tree. If you're looking for adventure, you can dive off an almost 50-foot (15-meter) waterfall (though a few backpackers have already snuffed it—more on page 175). Actually, Costa Rica has everything you could possibly want—if you ignore the fact that there's nothing much left of the original culture since the country began living mainly

EL ARENAL

SAN JOSÉ

Playa
Hermosa
Dominical

First we took a bus to the Arenal Volcano, a gigantic, prehistoric, smoking cone surrounded by jungle. At its foot, large, silvery lakes were sparkling in the sun. Mist had risen off the lakes and lay in thick blankets on the treetops. It was like being in *Jurassic Park*! As we walked through the jungle, we kept hearing the screeches of howler monkeys. These monkeys have unbelievable voice boxes—it's hard to believe they're only 1½ feet (0.5 meter) tall. Fun fact: Recordings of howler monkeys were actually used in the *Jurassic Park* movie to simulate the roaring of dinosaurs.

For an entire day we wandered through the jungle looking at toucans, finding hidden waterfalls, eating wild oranges off the trees. A local told us about a nearby river where hot volcanic water had created a sort of natural whirlpool you could actually sit in. That was exactly the type of thing we were looking for and sounded like the perfect ending to a day in the jungle. We bought ourselves some cold beers and took a cab to the river. Once we got there, the hot spring wasn't hard to find. As we climbed down the path to the riverbank, we were met by other backpackers going in the opposite direction. The place was indescribably beautiful: The river flowed quietly into two shallow, natural pools. We looked for a spot with the perfect temperature, plopped into the water, took a swig of cold beer, and relaxed. Some of the backpackers had placed candles on the rocks around the water. Nice.

From the volcano, we caught a rickety bus to Tamarindo. There we found some acceptable waves, but the real swell was absent. We wouldn't necessarily recommend this spot as a destination. There's already too much of a tourist infrastructure. There must be plenty of people in the world who like to visit small towns where they can sit on the beach drinking their lattes or macchiatos and ordering pizza, but we aren't among them. Instead, we bought some more or less affordable ingredients from the supermarket and made our own tasty pitas.

TICA PITA
COSTA RICAN PITA

One of our low-budget creations. Tastes great and is quick to make!

SERVES 2

2 WHOLE PITAS WITH POCKET OPENINGS
1 TABLESPOON VEGETABLE OIL
1 SMALL RED ONION, MINCED
2 CLOVES GARLIC, MINCED
8 OUNCES (250 G) GROUND BEEF
8 OUNCES (250 G) GROUND PORK
1 CUP (240 ML) WHITE WINE
1 BUNCH RADISHES, MINCED
1 BUNCH CILANTRO, MINCED
JUICE OF 1 LIME
PINCH OF GROUND CUMIN
SALT AND FRESHLY GROUND BLACK PEPPER
SEVERAL LETTUCE OR SPINACH LEAVES
1 AVOCADO
RUM KETCHUP (PAGE 50)

Preheat the oven to 400°F (200°C). Heat the pitas on a baking sheet for 10 to 12 minutes, until they gradually turn brown, become crispy, and puff up.

Heat the oil in a medium skillet over medium heat and cook the onion and garlic until the onion becomes translucent, 12 to 15 minutes.

Heat a second medium skillet over high heat. Add the ground beef and pork and brown it for about 15 minutes while breaking it up with a wooden spoon. Pour in the wine. Add the onions and garlic and cook for another 5 minutes.

In a bowl, mix together the ground meat mixture, radishes, and cilantro. Squeeze lime juice over the top, add the cumin, season with salt and pepper to taste, and let stand briefly.

Cut open the pitas along one side and line them with the lettuce. Peel and slice the avocado. Fill the pitas with the meat mixture and avocado slices. Top with a little ketchup and dig in!

AGUACATE RELLENO À LA BAILEY
BAILEY'S STUFFED AVOCADO

In Tamarindo we met Chris Bailey, a surfer from Perth, in western Australia. He not only shared his notes on Costa Rican surf spots, but he also showed us how to make his low-budget, no-tech version of a stuffed avocado. This power snack is exactly what you need to rebuild your strength after surfing.

SERVES 4

HERB MAYO
1 (8¾-OUNCE/250 G) JAR MAYONNAISE
(OR HOMEMADE, PAGE 51)
JUICE OF 1 LIME
1 TABLESPOON LIGHT BROWN SUGAR
1 TEASPOON GROUND CUMIN
1 BUNCH CILANTRO, MINCED
1 BUNCH MINT, MINCED
SALT AND FRESHLY GROUND BLACK PEPPER

AVOCADO-TUNA SALAD
1 (15-OUNCE/425 G) CAN CHICKPEAS
1 (10½-OUNCE/300 G) CAN CORN
1 BUNCH CILANTRO
1 (6½-OUNCE/185 G) CAN OIL-PACKED
TUNA, DRAINED
1 RED BELL PEPPER, SEEDED AND MINCED
2 RED CHILE PEPPERS, SEEDED AND
MINCED
10 (30 G) PITTED GREEN OLIVES,
COARSELY CHOPPED
SALT AND FRESHLY GROUND BLACK PEPPER
4 AVOCADOS

For the mayonnaise, mix together the mayonnaise, lime juice, sugar, cumin, cilantro, and mint in a bowl. Season with salt and pepper to taste. Set aside.

For the avocado-tuna salad, pour the chickpeas and corn into a strainer and drain well. Finely chop the cilantro with the stems. Separate the tuna by pulling it apart coarsely with a fork. Combine the chickpeas, corn, cilantro, tuna, bell pepper, chile peppers, olives, and salt and pepper to taste in a bowl and mix well.

Halve the avocados lengthwise, remove the pits, and carefully scoop the flesh out of the peel. To avoid damaging the peels, be sure to leave about ¼ inch (.05 cm) of flesh lining the peel. Dice the avocado flesh and add it to the other ingredients, along with about half the herb mayonnaise. Mix it all together thoroughly.

Fill the hollowed-out avocado peels with the salad and drizzle with the remaining mayonnaise. If you have any salad left over, you can either eat it as it is or refill the avocado peels, as we did.

COSTA RICAN CASADO

This is probably Costa Rica's most famous dish. It generally consists of a piece of meat or fish in a hearty sauce with rice, beans, and a simple salad. It looks simple, is simple to make, tastes simple—and is simply delicious! We've made some alterations to the recipe to help the *casado* (which means "married" in Spanish) reach its full potential.

SERVES 2

1 RED BELL PEPPER, SEEDED

1 LARGE YELLOW ONION, SLICED INTO EIGHTHS

1 CUP PLUS 2 TO 3 TABLESPOONS VEGETABLE OIL

1/3 CUP (100 G) TOMATO PASTE

4 CUPS (1 LITER) CHICKEN STOCK, PLUS MORE IF NEEDED

1/2 CUP (120 ML) SALSA LIZANO OR

1/4 CUP (60 ML) WORCESTERSHIRE SAUCE

10 WHOLE BLACK PEPPERCORNS

4 BAY LEAVES

1 TABLESPOON PAPRIKA

1 TABLESPOON HONEY

ZEST AND JUICE OF 1 LIME

2 LARGE SKINLESS CHICKEN THIGHS

1 CUP (200 G) WHITE RICE

2 1/3 CUPS (450 G) CANNED BLACK BEANS

SALT AND FRESHLY GROUND BLACK PEPPER

SEVERAL SPRIGS CILANTRO, CHOPPED

1 RIPE PLANTAIN

1 TABLESPOON BROWN CANE SUGAR

Cut the red bell pepper into diamond-shaped pieces. Separate the onion layers.

In a large pot, heat 2 to 3 tablespoons oil over medium heat and cook the bell pepper and onion until tender, about 7 to 10 minutes. Add the tomato paste and brown for 1 minute while stirring. Add the stock and Salsa Lizano. Finally, add the peppercorns, bay leaves, paprika, honey, and lime juice, and stir well.

Place the chicken thighs in the pot, making sure that the meat is completely covered by liquid! If necessary, add more stock. Cover the pot and simmer the chicken over medium heat for about 45 minutes, or until cooked through.

In a second medium stockpot, combine the rice and 1¾ cups (420 ml) water, cover, and simmer over low heat until done. Add the beans, including the liquid from the can, and stir. Add the lime zest and season the rice-bean mixture with salt and black pepper to taste. Sprinkle it with the cilantro and set aside.

Peel the plantain and cut it diagonally into 1-inch-thick (3 cm) slices. Heat the remaining 1 cup oil in a pot over medium-high heat and fry the plantain slices for 15 minutes. Remove the slices from the oil, pat them dry with paper towels, and flatten them with a heavy glass. Return these plantain chips to the pot and fry them for another 5 minutes. Pat them dry with paper towels and place them in a bowl. Sprinkle them with the sugar and salt and black pepper to taste and toss them briefly.

Arrange the chicken, rice, beans, and plantains on a plate. It's best to mix them all together—just like the ticos and ticas do!

SLOW FOOD

MONTEZUMA

We continued on to Montezuma, a little spot on the Nicoya Peninsula embedded between the jungle and the beach. Montezuma can best be described as a small hippie community, with incense and homemade drums being sold on every corner. On the beach itself, we found a turtle hatchery that protected baby turtles and a place that sold fresh coconuts. We felt right at home in the Downtown Montezuma Hostel. Owner Elena and company provided us with fresh fish, cooked and ate it with us, and revealed to us their favorite ceviche recipe (see page 178).

In Costa Rica—as with everywhere else—we were looking for adventure, so we took a little walk into the jungle, where there were supposed to be several high waterfalls that were good for diving off. First, however, we had to scramble along a slope beside a brook and cross the brook several times before arriving at the waterfalls, which were deep in the jungle. In a small clearing, the water thundered down from about 130 feet (40 meters) above us. We climbed vertically alongside the waterfall, grabbing hold of tree roots as we went. Just as I was about to use a knothole as a handhold, I suddenly heard Cozy yelling at me from below. At the very last moment I saw why: The knothole was already occupied! A fist-size, shiny blue tarantula stared back at me. Startled, I temporarily lost my grip but in the nick of time found a vine I could grab onto. Ugh, that was close. A little more cautiously now, we clambered up the last 6½ feet (2 meters) to the top of the waterfall. Once there, we saw that this was only one of three waterfalls, although it was the tallest. We'd heard that it was possible to dive off a second waterfall that was almost 50 feet (15 meters) high. Supposedly several people had already died trying, but we decided to risk it anyway. We stood on the brink, took deep breaths, and simultaneously plunged headlong into the unknown. The adrenaline rush while we were falling through the air was unbelievable—as was the impact. Luckily, the water was deep enough, and when we returned to the surface we were shouting with relief. We felt no need to try our luck a second time, however, so instead we climbed deeper into the jungle, farther and farther uphill, until we finally discovered a deserted platform high in the treetops. Scrambling onto it, we ate the bananas we'd picked on the way and enjoyed the view over the jungle to the ocean. Montezuma was good to us.

CEVICHE

Finally we come to ceviche, THE culinary discovery of our trip: refreshing, light, satisfying, healthy, and multifaceted. This dish originated in Peru, the mecca of ceviche. We found some form of ceviche in every country we visited, from Mexico to Chile, so it's worth starting out with a little general information before moving on to the actual recipes.

Ceviche is raw fish or seafood marinated in citrus juice, most often lime juice (*leche de tigre*—"tiger's milk"). The acidity of the lime juice sets in motion a process by which the proteins are denatured, similar to heating. The consistency and color of the fish slowly changes. The flesh turns white and its texture becomes firmer. The longer the fish marinates in the lime juice, the more "well-done" it becomes.

When buying the fish, be absolutely certain to ask for sushi-quality fish, because ceviche, like sushi, depends on freshness and high-quality ingredients. Also make sure the fish is well refrigerated and that you prepare and serve it as soon as possible.

The types of fish used for ceviche can be divided into three categories. Firm fish, such as cod and hake, requires more time in the tiger's milk than medium-firm fish such as halibut, tuna, salmon, and some types of perch. Softer fish, such as mullet and mackerel, needs to marinate only half as long as fish with a firmer texture.

The way in which ceviche is prepared depends on the region. In some countries, it's common to marinate the fish in the sour citrus juice for an hour before serving. In Mexico the fish is first cut into pieces, then marinated in lime juice, and finally chopped in a food processor together with onions, carrots, chile peppers, and cilantro before being served on crisp, deep-fried tortillas. In Peru, there's no marinating to speak of: The ceviche is served immediately after preparation.

In its simplest form, ceviche is composed of only five essential ingredients: the freshest raw fish, lime juice, thin strips of red onion, salt, and pepper. Once you've established these basics, however, the sky's the limit: Polynesian ceviche with diced mango, cilantro, and coconut milk; salmon ceviche with star fruit, green apples, and ginger syrup; octopus ceviche with chile peppers and celery; authentic bonito ceviche with mandarin orange segments; brook trout ceviche with honeydew melon and pomegranate seeds—the possibilities are endless! We recommend that you start with the basic version on page 250 so you can get a feel for the dish and its components. Now head for the fresh fish counter!

BONITO CEVICHE ON BEET CARPACCIO

We drove with Elena to surf at Santa Teresa. On the way back, we stopped in a little village with a fishing harbor and bought ultra-fresh bonito right off the boat. For the next few days, we ate fish! First, of course, we had ceviche—in this case using Elena's favorite recipe with beet carpaccio and an Asian dressing of soy sauce and ginger. Check it out!

SERVES 4

GINGER SYRUP
1 HAZELNUT-SIZE PIECE FRESH GINGER, PEELED AND GRATED
1/4 CUP (4 TABLESPOONS) MAPLE SYRUP
1 TABLESPOON SOY SAUCE

CEVICHE
1 OR 2 MEDIUM OR LARGE BEETS, COOKED AND COOLED
1/4 CUP (4 TABLESPOONS) OLIVE OIL
FRESHLY GROUND BLACK PEPPER
2 1/4 POUNDS (1 KG) ULTRA-FRESH BONITO OR
YELLOWFIN TUNA
1 BUNCH SCALLIONS, THINLY SLICED
1/2 BUNCH PARSLEY, CHOPPED
SEA SALT
1 CUP (240 ML) LIME JUICE
LIME WEDGES, FOR GARNISH

To make the ginger syrup, combine the ginger, maple syrup, and soy sauce. Set aside.

To make the ceviche, using a sharp knife, cut the beet into paper-thin slices. You can also use the slicing side of a box grater or similar tool. (The main thing is that you end up with nice, uniformly thin slices.)

Arrange the beet slices in an overlapping pattern on serving plates, drizzle them with the ginger syrup and olive oil, and season them with pepper to taste.

Cut the fish into 1/2-inch (1.5 cm) cubes. In a bowl, mix together the fish, scallions, parsley, and salt and pepper to taste. Squeeze the lime juice over the top, gently stir well, and distribute the ceviche over the beets. Serve with lime wedges on the side. Bon appétit!

FAST FOOD

FRIED FISH FILLET
ON KABOCHA SAUCE
WITH GREEN RICE

From the tourist town of Tamarindo, we fled to the quieter Montezuma. There, too, we found innumerable fishermen selling fresh fish and a well-stocked market with countless vegetables. Unfortunately there were no waves, so we spent the day cooking instead.

SERVES 4

KABOCHA SAUCE
1/2 KABOCHA SQUASH
1 TABLESPOON SALTED BUTTER
1 CLOVE GARLIC, MINCED
1 YELLOW BELL PEPPER, SEEDED AND CHOPPED COARSELY
1 INCH (2.5 CM) FRESH GINGER, PEELED AND GRATED
1 RED CHILE PEPPER, SEEDED AND MINCED
3/4 CUP (180 ML) COCONUT MILK
1 TEASPOON GROUND MUSTARD
1 TEASPOON GROUND CUMIN
JUICE OF 1 LIME
2 TEASPOONS BROWN CANE SUGAR
SALT AND FRESHLY GROUND BLACK PEPPER

GREEN RICE
1 TEASPOON SALT
2 CUPS (400 G) WHITE RICE
SALSA VERDE (PAGE 50)

FISH
UNSALTED BUTTER, FOR BROWNING
4 WHITE FISH FILLETS (SUCH AS COD, SOLE, OR TILAPIA)
SALT AND FRESHLY GROUND BLACK PEPPER
LIME WEDGES, FOR SERVING

To make the kabocha sauce, cut the unpeeled squash into large pieces. Melt the butter in a medium pot. As soon as it starts to foam, brown the squash pieces, garlic, bell pepper, ginger, and chile pepper for 5 minutes while stirring. Add the coconut milk. Add 1 cup (240 ml) water, the ground mustard, and the cumin, and simmer for 20 minutes. As soon as the squash is soft enough that you can pierce it fairly easily with a knife, purée the entire mixture in a blender or food processor. Add the lime juice and sugar, and season with salt and pepper to taste.

To make the green rice, bring 3¾ cups (900 ml) water to a boil. Add the salt and rice, cover, and simmer for 30 to 35 minutes. When the rice is done, mix it with the salsa verde.

To make the fish, melt the butter in a skillet over medium heat and brown the fillets for about 5 minutes per side, or until they're crisp and golden brown. Season them with salt and pepper to taste.

Spoon a little kabocha sauce onto each plate and place a serving of rice on top. Top the rice with a piece of fish and a lime wedge.

TROPICAL PANCAKES

The best breakfast ever. If you really want to impress, serve these pancakes for breakfast in bed.

SERVES 2

PASSION FRUIT–YOGURT SAUCE

2 PASSION FRUITS
2¼ CUPS (500 G) PLAIN YOGURT
3 TABLESPOONS HONEY

MANGO-COCONUT SAUCE

1 RIPE MANGO, PEELED AND DICED
⅔ CUP (160 ML) UNSWEETENED COCONUT MILK
1 TEASPOON GROUND CINNAMON

GINGER SYRUP

½ INCH (1.5 CM) FRESH GINGER, PEELED AND GRATED
2 TO 3 TABLESPOONS MAPLE SYRUP

PANCAKES

2 CUPS (240 G) ALL–PURPOSE FLOUR
1 TABLESPOON (11 GRAMS) BAKING POWDER
2 TABLESPOONS SUGAR
PINCH OF SALT
2 MEDIUM EGGS
1¼ CUPS (300 ML) MILK
5 TABLESPOONS VEGETABLE OIL
4 TEASPOONS SALTED BUTTER
2 BANANAS, SLICED

TOPPINGS

VARIOUS FRUITS CUT INTO PIECES, GRATED CHOCOLATE, FRESH MINT LEAVES (OPTIONAL), AND AN APPETITE!

For the passion fruit–yogurt sauce, halve the passion fruits and scrape out the flesh with a spoon. Stir together the passion fruit, yogurt, and honey in a bowl. Set aside.

For the mango-coconut sauce, in a bowl using a handheld blender, blend the mango with the coconut milk and cinnamon until creamy. Set aside.

For the ginger syrup, stir the ginger and maple syrup together in a small bowl. Set aside.

To make the pancakes, combine the flour, baking powder, sugar, and salt in a medium bowl. In another medium bowl, whisk together the eggs and milk. Whisk the oil into the egg-milk mixture. Add the flour mixture to the liquid mixture a little at a time while stirring. Let the batter stand for about 10 minutes. So easy!

To cook the pancakes, heat the butter in a skillet or on a griddle and ladle on 3 to 4 tablespoons of the batter per pancake. Press several banana slices into each pancake while the batter is still liquid, before flipping them. Only flip the pancakes once you see small bubbles forming around the circumference of the cakes; this should take about 3 to 5 minutes per pancake depending on your flame and the size of your cakes. Gradually cook all the pancakes, arrange them on plates, and top them with the sauces and fruits as desired.

COSTA RICA SURF GUIDE

Admittedly, we didn't visit many surf spots in Costa Rica. At the time there was a lull in the swell. We had good waves in Santa Teresa and Tamarindo, but none really worth recommending or worth a trip. A visit to Witch's Rock would probably have been worthwhile, but the only way to reach it was by boat for $100—money we didn't have. This surf guide was written by our Australian friend Chris, whom we first met in Tamarindo and whom we ran into repeatedly during our trip south. You can see him on page 170.

TAMARINDO 10.30521°N –85.83996°E

Tamarindo claims to be an important Costa Rican surf city, but in fact it has everything except good waves. The beach break is protected from the southern swell and is usually packed with beginners. If you travel south toward Langosta, you'll find more stable conditions for surfing that are best at mid to high tide. Then you have good waves with almost every swell, even if they don't have a lot of power.

Playa Grande, in northern Tamarindo on the other side of the river mouth, is much more exposed to the southern swell. It can be surfed at any tide, but the quality of the spot is highly dependent on sandbanks. Even if it's not great for surfing, Tamarindo is a good point of departure for learning about some of Central America's highlights, such as Witch's Rock and Ollie's Point. Talk to the local surf guides to help plan your trip. Although these spots are fairly remote, they're super when there's a solid southern swell.

DOMINICAL 9.24919°N –83.87066°E

One of the better surf spots along Costa Rica's Pacific coast. The quality of the wave depends a lot on the sand banks. If the wave here gets too big, try the left 1¼ miles (2 kilometers) to the south, which can often be surfed all day. The people on this beach are nicely spread out. It has many small peaks and a strong current from the north that pushes against the river mouth. (Note: There are said to be crocodiles here.) Because the wind doesn't do the waves any good during the day, you should come here in the morning or late afternoon.

PLAYA HERMOSA 9.55877°N –84.58340°E

This beach is 5 miles (5 kilometers) south of Jaco. One of Costa Rica's most famous waves breaks here, with a barrel that's famous for breaking boards and backs. Dependent on the swell and movement in the sandy bottom but independent of tide.

PUNTARENAS

SANTA TERESA 9.64293°N –85.17056°E

This is another typical Costa Rican surfer town with lots of surfers but only mediocre surfing conditions. The best spot is toward the La Lara bar, where there are higher waves and fewer rocks. Regardless of the swell, the waves here are best at mid to high tide.

Take the short trip south to Playa Hermosa, where you'll find better conditions with a long left over a mixture of rocks and sand. Best at mid tide and early in the morning before the wind picks up. Although there are lots of people in the water, there are enough waves to go around.

PAVONES 8.38963°N –83.14058°E

This is an essential stop for anyone traveling in Central America. The wave is supposed to be the second longest left in the world and is more for pros. It breaks over gravel at a river mouth. The greatest difficulty here—apart from the crowds—is figuring out the right time to surf. You need a solid swell of at least 5 feet (1.5 meters) and a period of about 17 seconds. It must come from about 200° from the south-southwest. When all these factors come together, Pavones can give you the wave of your life—easy takeoff followed by a few excellent sections and large walls.

SEE VIDEO:

Bocas del Toro

Santa Catalina

Playa Venao

SAN BLAS

PANAMA CITY

OH, how beaut...but no, it would be too easy to start the chapter that way. Still, we were eager to find out whether Panama would live up to our childhood dreams inspired by Janosch. (Janosch is a German children's author who wrote a book called *Oh, wie schön ist Panama* [*Oh, How Beautiful Is Panama*].) We'll give you a hint: It did! With the San Blas Islands and Bocas del Toro Archipelago, Panama contains some very special Caribbean jewels just waiting to be discovered. Even the famous Panama Canal is worth a visit, as is the nightlife in Panama City. There are wonderful spots on the Pacific side, as well, such as Playa Venao and the famous wave of Santa Catalina.

But first we had to cross the border, which was an experience in itself: Carrying heavy packs, we shuffled across the brittle wooden planks of an old pedestrian bridge that spans the Sixaola River between Costa Rica and Panama. This river is a constant source of tension between the two countries. It keeps changing its course and shifting the border, so that a farmer's field might be in Costa Rica one day and in Panama the next.

When we reached the other shore, a small, wobbly bus took us to a taxi boat that was sailing to Bocas del Toro, a Caribbean island paradise with crystal-clear water and a Rastafarian flair. Once again we were extremely lucky. Normally there aren't any waves here in September, but one peek at the reef break known as Tiger Tails told us that the opposite was true—we found perfect Caribbean barrels from shoulder to head height. We got butterflies in our stomachs—it was love at first sight!

PANAMA SURF GUIDE

BOCAS DEL TORO

Although we found good waves in Bocas del Toro in the middle of August, it wasn't exactly Caribbean-wave season. The best waves are from December to March and in June and July.

TIGER TAILS 9.36742°N -82.23847°E

The Tiger Tails reef break was just around the corner from where we were staying, at the Pukalani Hostel, and directly in front of a surf bar. A fast, hollow right and a left that's a little harder to surf.

PAUNCH REEF 9.38069°N -82.23631°E

A reef/point break, not a beginner wave. Fast, hollow tubes in the first section, then a less steep section.

BLUFF BEACH 9.39728°N -82.24348°E

This spot is on a picturesque jungle beach. It's a beach break with lots of peaks that are more or less directly exposed to the swell. Generally the waves break fairly close to shore, so you'll have to accept a thorough soaking. Sand in the butt crack is guaranteed.

PLAYA VENAO 7.43150°N -80.19522°E

A long beach break with loads of peaks. Fantastic for beginners, but even experienced surfers can get their money's worth. We had all kinds of fun at this spot!

SANTA CATALINA 7.62299°N -81.25072°E

La Punta has become one of the most famous waves in Central America—and for good reason. This spot is extremely consistent and truly massive. But you'll never have it to yourself, at least not when the weather forecast is good. The best waves are from April to October, but there's actually good surfing year-round.

TIGER TAILS

BLUFF

e spent our weeks in Panama cooking, surfing, and taking photos, in typical Salt & Silver style. Even when we weren't looking for new ingredients or recipes, we stumbled onto them. In Santa Catalina we bought four freshly caught giant lobsters for less than $15 from a half-blind fisherman when all we'd really meant to do was ask for directions. A few hours later we'd transformed them into crisp brown grilled Lobster Tails with Lemon-Garlic Butter, accompanied by creamy spaghetti nests with a beet-horseradish sauce. As we stuffed our faces and sat on our roof terrace looking out over the Santa Catalina point break, we were glad we'd been forced to ask for directions.

LOBSTER TAILS WITH LEMON-GARLIC BUTTER

SERVES 2

3 LOBSTERS
3 TABLESPOONS COCONUT OIL
SALT
3 TABLESPOONS UNSALTED BUTTER
2 TABLESPOONS OLIVE OIL
3 CLOVES GARLIC, MINCED

JUICE OF 3 LEMONS
1 TEASPOON RED PEPPER FLAKES
1 BUNCH CILANTRO, MINCED
PINCH OF SUGAR
FRESHLY GROUND BLACK PEPPER

196

PANAMA

Detach the lobster tails and cut them in half lengthwise (reserve the claws for another use). Rub them with a mixture of coconut oil and a little salt. Heat a large, ungreased pan. (The lobster tails are already greased.) Brown the lobster tails, cut side down, in the pan for 5 minutes on each side, or until golden-brown.

To prepare the garlic butter, melt the butter in a small saucepan over low heat, add the olive oil, and stir. As soon as the butter starts to foam slightly, add the garlic and braise it for 5 minutes. Do not let it turn brown or burn!

Add the lemon juice, red pepper flakes, and cilantro to the saucepan, stir, and transfer the butter to a small bowl. Season the butter with sugar, salt, and pepper to taste.

Serve the lobster tails with the lemon-garlic butter and the following pasta:

PASTA WITH BEET-HORSERADISH SAUCE

SERVES 2

10 OUNCES (300 G) LINGUINE
½ CUP (100 G) COOKED BEETS FINELY GRATED ON A BOX GRATER
⅓ CUP (100 G) CRÈME FRAÎCHE
3 TABLESPOONS HOT HORSERADISH FROM A JAR
1 TEASPOON DIJON MUSTARD
1 TABLESPOON UNSALTED BUTTER
1 TEASPOON HONEY
SALT AND FRESHLY GROUND BLACK PEPPER

Bring a large pot of water to a boil. Cook the linguine according to the directions on the package until it's al dente.

Meanwhile, combine the beets, crème fraîche, horseradish, and mustard in a medium pot and stir well. Heat the sauce over low heat, stirring occasionally, for 7 to 10 minutes. Remove the sauce from the heat and purée it.

Just before the linguine's done, add the butter and honey to the sauce and season it with salt and pepper to taste.

Using a pasta fork, transfer the linguine directly to the sauce and mix well in a large bowl. We recommend that you serve it with the Lobster Tails with Lemon-Garlic Butter (see above).

FAST FOOD

Next stop: Playa Venao. There we found a wonderful hostel called Eco Venao that had its own rain forest reforestation project, outstanding food, and small villas where we could live like kings at hostel prices. The kitchen, which was open to the jungle and the ocean, inspired in us some extremely promising recipes—due in large part to the fact that every afternoon a pickup truck delivered huge crates of freshly caught tuna. Because the most important factor in preparing ceviche (see page 176) is the freshness and quality of the fish, and because these fish were being unloaded right under our very noses, we immediately knew what we needed to make.

MANDARIN ORANGE CEVICHE

You can make this dish with fish other than bonito, such as yellowfin tuna, but make sure the flesh isn't too firm. Raw fish shouldn't require a lot of chewing. It should melt in your mouth! Ask your fishmonger for the freshest fish. A good seller will show you the whole fish, scale and skin it, fillet it, and remove the bones. A top-quality fish has crystal-clear eyes and bright-red gills and doesn't smell fishy. The less it stinks, the fresher it is!

SERVES 2

2 MANDARIN ORANGES
1 SMALL RED ONION
4 INCHES (10 CM) LEEK
14 OUNCES (400 G) ULTRA-FRESH BONITO FILLETS, WELL CHILLED
JUICE OF 4 LIMES
JUICE OF 2 LEMONS
SALT AND FRESHLY GROUND BLACK PEPPER

Peel the mandarin oranges and cut the individual segments in half lengthwise. (Extra credit: Remove the outer membranes, too, and the ceviche will be even more delicious.) Place them in a bowl.

Peel the onion, taking off the outer two or three layers and keeping only the tender inner layers. Cut the heart of the onion in half and then cut it into paper-thin strips. (A trick for taking some of the bite out of raw onion slices: Sprinkle them with 1 teaspoon salt and 1 teaspoon sugar, mix them all together, and let them stand for 5 minutes. Finally, rinse off the salt and sugar.) Rinse and clean the leek and cut it into fine rings. Place the onion and leek in the bowl with the oranges.

Using an extremely sharp knife, cut the fish into ¾-inch (2 cm) cubes and add it to the bowl. Pour the lime and lemon juice over the top and gently toss to combine everything. Season with salt and pepper to taste and toss again. Serve immediately! This goes well with toasted white bread.

For a change of scenery, we took a night bus to Panama City and woke up the next morning at six o'clock, just as the sun was coming up and the bus was crossing the Panama Canal. Giant container ships were entering the locks and being lowered 65 feet (20 meters) in less than a quarter of an hour. The morning mist was disappearing among the city's skyscrapers. We moved into the Panamericana Hostel in the Casco Viejo quarter and enjoyed a fantastic view from the roof terrace. As we sat with beers in hand, taking in the scenery, we suddenly realized it was time to get some more tattoos. A quick glance online told us that The Rock Spot tattoo shop was currently hosting an excellent, traditional tattoo artist from Mexico. We phoned, made an appointment, and were soon in the presence of Moisés Jiménez, from Mexico City. Beneath his eye he'd tattooed a crescent moon, his signature, which he somehow inserts into almost all his tattoos. Cozy expanded his collection of kitchen appliances to include a chef's knife on his leg and, just for the heck of it, a dagger on his thumb. I opted for a mandala on the inside of my upper arm. Why not?

From Panama City, we booked a three-day trip to the San Blas Islands, home of the Kuna Yala native people and picture-perfect, travel-brochure scenery, with white sandy beaches and turquoise-blue water. San Blas is comprised of lots of little islands, most of which are no bigger than a football field. You can walk their entire shoreline in five minutes. Other than bamboo huts for sleeping, white sand, and coconut palms, there's nothing there—but what more could a person need? Beach volleyball and snorkeling were our favorite pastimes, and the Kuna Yala's abundant supply of rum made the evenings fun. The one bad thing about San Blas is that the indigenous culture is completely gone. Almost all the beautiful islands are reserved for tourists, who are constantly arriving in groups of ten for two days at a time. The Kuna Yala themselves live only on the two main islands, in dirty, cramped villages from which they manage their island realm.

A visit to the islands isn't exactly cheap. Food and lodging are definitely for-profit. Morning, noon, and night we were offered a medium serving of fried fish or chicken with white rice or French fries, plus a side salad—you know the type: iceberg lettuce, tomato, and vinegar. We dreamed of discovering some otherworldly, ancient native recipes, but this time we were out of luck. We tried everything we could think of to wheedle a few secret, traditional recipes out of the usually tipsy island chef, and at one point thought we'd done it. When we showed an

interest in the finer points of Kuna Yala cuisine, his eyes lit up and he told us about the fantastic lobsters that had always been available on the islands. He would prepare some especially for us! We were rubbing our hands together in anticipation of a rum-coconut sauce with ginger or something similar. He wouldn't let us watch him in the kitchen, so we waited patiently outside. When he finally came out half an hour later, he served us... lobster with French fries and ketchup, with a little iceberg lettuce and a tomato slice languishing on the side. That'll be 23 euros ($25), please.

After we got back to Panama City, we consoled ourselves with the most decadent burgers ever. Give yourself a treat!

Woooow...not.

PANAMA BURGERS

WITH HOMEMADE BUNS

Preparing the buns takes time, but there's really no comparison between the homemade version and the raggedy hamburger buns you'll find in a supermarket.

MAKES 8 BURGERS

BUNS

¾ CUP (180 ML) LUKEWARM WATER, AT 105°F (40°C)

3 TABLESPOONS WARM MILK

2 TABLESPOONS SUGAR

3½ TABLESPOONS (42 G) FRESH YEAST

2 MEDIUM EGGS

3⅓ CUPS (425 G) ALL-PURPOSE FLOUR

⅓ CUP (60 G) TYPE "00" FLOUR

2 TEASPOONS SALT

5½ TABLESPOONS (80 G) UNSALTED BUTTER, SOFTENED

BLACK SESAME SEEDS, FOR SPRINKLING

To make the dough for the buns, stir together the water, milk, and sugar. Add the yeast to the mixture and stir well. Let the mixture stand for 15 minutes.

Whisk one of the eggs and set aside. Combine the two types of flour and the salt in a large bowl. Add the butter and knead everything together to make a fine, crumbly dough. Then add the yeast mixture and the whisked egg. Roll up your sleeves and knead the dough vigorously for 8 to 10 minutes on a floured surface, until it has a silky shine. Place the dough in a bowl, cover it with a kitchen towel, and let it rise for about 1 hour.

Line a baking sheet with parchment paper. Shape the dough into 8 equal-size buns and place them on the baking sheet. Let them rise on the baking sheet for 1 hour.

Preheat the oven to 390°F (200°C) and place a small ovenproof bowl filled with water on the oven floor.

Whisk the second egg with a little water and brush it onto the buns. Finally, sprinkle the buns with sesame seeds and put them in the oven. Bake them for just 15 minutes and you've done it!

→

PATTIES

2 HANDFULS CORNFLAKES
1 TEASPOON GROUND CUMIN
1 TEASPOON WHOLE BLACK PEPPERCORNS
1 LARGE YELLOW ONION, MINCED
2¼ POUNDS (1 KG) GROUND BEEF
1 LARGE EGG YOLK

TOPPINGS

1 PAPAYA
1 TABLESPOON COCONUT OIL
1 COOKED BEET, THINLY SLICED
8 SLICES TANGY CHEESE OF YOUR CHOICE
1 AVOCADO
BARBECUE SAUCE (PAGE 114)
SALSA VERDE (PAGE 50)
CHIPOTLE–LIME SAUCE (PAGE 51), MIXED
WITH 1 MASHED BANANA

To make the patties, crush the cornflakes finely in a mortar and pestle. Crush the cumin and peppercorns in a mortar and pestle. In a large bowl, knead together all of the ingredients for the patties. Shape the mixture into 8 equal-size burgers. Remember that they'll shrink when they're cooked, so make them a little larger and flatter than necessary.

Preheat the oven to 150°F (70°C) or the lowest setting possible. Peel the papaya and cut it into slices ⅓ inch (1 cm) thick. Heat the coconut oil in a skillet and brown the papaya and beet slices over high heat in batches until they turn a nice golden brown. Transfer them to an ovenproof plate and keep them warm in the oven.

Now fry the burger patties in the very hot pan. Turn them and lift them up with a spatula after a few minutes to make sure they don't burn. If you think the outsides of the burgers are getting too brown, just decrease the heat. Altogether the burgers need a good 10 to 15 minutes to become crusty on the outside and medium inside. It's hard to say exactly how much time on each side— it depends on how hot the pan is, the meat itself, the thickness of the burgers, and the mood of the burger gods! Around 15 minutes should be ideal, or a little bit longer if you prefer them more well-done. To make sure all the burgers are done at the same time, try frying them in two pans simultaneously. Place a cheese slice on top of each burger.

Peel the avocado, remove the pit, and cut the flesh into slices. Cut the hamburger buns in half crosswise and build a tower with the toppings: First spread a little barbecue sauce on the bottom half of each bun. Add a burger, then beet slices, and then papaya slices. Place a dollop of salsa in the center of the papaya slices. Then add the avocado slices. Last of all, spread the top half of the bun with a thick layer of the banana-chipotle mixture and place it on top.

For Cozy's birthday we treated ourselves to something really special: a double room in a luxury hotel. Oh boy! After months of sleeping in hammocks, on stone benches, in stinking six-person bedrooms, on car seats, in bunk beds, or sharing a small, hard mattress, we set our sights on a little luxury and booked a room on the twentieth floor of the Trump Ocean Club. In the middle of the room was a freestanding bathtub. There were plush bathrobes with a gold embroidered Trump logo and two massive, soft, king-size beds. We settled into the hotel restaurant and ordered two enormous steaks with red wine–shallot sauce and then slept a deep sleep. It was the best possible ending to our Panama episode. The next day, we flew to Ecuador.

ECUADOR

SEE VIDEO:

Mompiche

Canoa

Puerto Lopéz

GUAYAQUIL

Galápagos

QUITO

n Quito we took our first steps on South American soil. Quito is 9,350 feet (2,850 meters) above sea level, roughly the height of the Zugspitze (the highest mountain in Germany). The difference in temperature compared to Caribbean Panama is just as great. It was the first time on our trip that we ran into an old acquaintance: snow! We weren't exactly prepared for it as we stepped off the plane in our flip-flops and board shorts.

Quito couldn't be called a safe place. For the first few days we had no idea what areas to avoid because whenever we ventured outside the main tourist zone, locals came running up to us in a panic shouting, "*Cuidado! Cuidado!*" In other words, "Be careful! Be careful!" When we asked what we were supposed to be careful of, we always got the same answer: Just two days ago in this very street "they" attacked someone. So naturally it left us wondering if we should be climbing that particular ghetto hill.

Fortunately, old friends had put us in touch with some graffiti artists in Quito. We met up with them and immediately got on great. Night after night we partied, ate, and painted. In the company of these artists, we suddenly had no problem strolling through Quito's "barrios" at night. Without meaning to, we'd probably become part of the gang that other people were crossing the street to avoid. But the best possible thing happened after we'd been in Quito for a few days: The Ecuadorians accepted us into their crew. Salt & Silver joined ALM, one of the best graffiti crews in the country. We were now members of the family and signed all our paintings with the crew's tag. To seal the deal, we were invited to design a giant Salt & Silver wall in honor of the opening of a new architecture, design, and illustration studio. So we hung with the crew—literally, because while we painted, we hung 49 feet (15 meters) in the air, holding on by one hand to a wobbly, windblown iron-bar construction. Yeah, well, everything comes at a...

After seven hours of climbing, painting, and freezing our butts off, we were done in every sense of the word. Fortunately, the guys' favorite empanada shop was right around the corner. Hot pockets were just what we needed.

EMPANADAS

EMPANADAS

The name means "wrapped in dough." You can find this typical Latin American specialty everywhere in one form or another, from northern Mexico to Tierra del Fuego. As for the fillings, use your imagination. Whether you use seasoned puréed vegetables, ground meat, or mushrooms, you can't go wrong.

DOUGH

MAKES 16 EMPANADAS

1¾ CUPS (250 G) WHOLE WHEAT FLOUR
1½ CUPS (250 G) FINE YELLOW CORNMEAL
1 TABLESPOON SUGAR
1 TABLESPOON SALT
⅓ CUP (100 G) MARGARINE, MELTED
1⅓ TABLESPOONS (20 ML) OLIVE OIL
⅔ CUP (160 ML) LUKEWARM WATER,
AT 105°F (40°C)
1⅓ TABLESPOONS (20 ML) MILK
1 LARGE EGG

In a large bowl, combine the flour, cornmeal, sugar, and salt and make a well in the center. Place the margarine, olive oil, water, milk, and egg in the center of a well in the middle of the dry ingredients. Knead until you have a smooth, uniform dough—the process is extremely quick and easy. Chill the dough for several hours. Then cover it and let it warm to room temperature for 30 minutes before proceeding.

While the dough's warming up, prepare the fillings.

EMPANADAS DE CARNE Y QUESO
MEAT AND CHEESE

3 TABLESPOONS VEGETABLE OIL
1 CARROT, PEELED AND DICED
1 SMALL RED ONION, DICED
1 POUND (500 G) GROUND BEEF
1⅓ CUPS (200 G) FETA CHEESE
2 CLOVES GARLIC
⅔ CUP (100 G) PITTED KALAMATA OLIVES,
CHOPPED
1 TEASPOON GROUND CUMIN
SALT AND FRESHLY GROUND BLACK PEPPER

Heat the oil in a skillet over medium heat, and sauté the carrot and onion in the oil for several minutes. Add the meat and brown everything together for about 10 minutes. Then turn off the heat and crumble the feta over the meat. Peel the garlic and squeeze it through a press. Add the olives, garlic, and cumin, and season with salt and pepper to taste. Stir the mixture for another 1 to 2 minutes so that the cheese melts and becomes evenly distributed. Let the mixture cool slightly before filling the empanadas (see right).

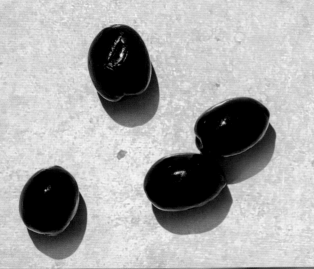

EMPANADAS DE CAMARONES Y YUCA
SHRIMP AND CASSAVA

3½ TABLESPOONS (50 G) BUTTER
14 OUNCES (400 G) SMALL SHRIMP, PEELED
AND DEVEINED
2 CLOVES GARLIC, THINLY SLICED
1 RED CHILE PEPPER, SEEDED AND MINCED
2⅔ CUPS (400 G) COOKED CASSAVA ROOT
OR POTATOES, DICED
2 HANDFULS CILANTRO, CHOPPED
SALT AND FRESHLY GROUND BLACK PEPPER

Melt the butter in a skillet over medium heat and sauté the shrimp, garlic, chile, and cassava root or potatoes in the butter until the shrimp are cooked and the potatoes, if used, are a little crumbly. The whole thing should resemble very lumpy mashed potatoes with shrimp. Stir in the cilantro and season with salt and pepper to taste—that's all it takes to make this phenomenal empanada filling.

FILLING THE EMPANADAS

When you've finished making the fillings, let them cool a little while you roll and cut the dough.

Preheat the oven to 400°F (200°C). Line a baking sheet with parchment paper.

Roll out half the dough on a floured work surface to a thickness of ⅛ inch (3 mm). Cut out circles of dough using a round cookie cutter (about 4½ inches/12 cm in diameter) or a bowl. Place 1 heaping tablespoon of filling in the center of each circle. Fold the dough once in half in the middle and press the edges together with a fork. There really isn't much that can go wrong—with just a little practice, you'll be making beautiful empanadas!

Arrange the empanadas on the prepared baking sheet and bake them for just 15 to 20 minutes—and that's it! If you want, you can whisk an egg yolk and brush it onto the empanadas before baking to give them a nice golden crust. *Buen provecho!*

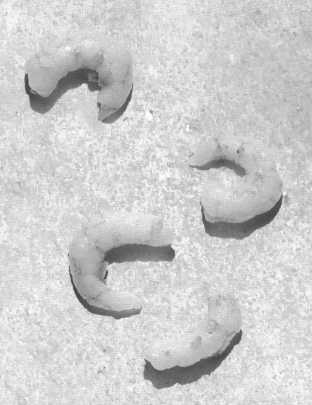

After spending time in Quito, we'd had enough of the wind and weather and headed for the beach. We caught a bus to Atacames, which was supposed to be a nice surf spot. Bullshit! It was a randomly cemented-together collection of tourist bunkers with a beach full of umbrellas suspended over package tourists getting plastered on cheap cocktails. We put up with it for exactly half a day and then took off for Mompiche, several hours to the south of Atacames. Mompiche was much more our style. A black lava beach, fishing boats, shelters resembling tree houses made of bamboo and wood. Cool. The only bad thing: There was nowhere we could pay with a credit card and there were no ATMs. Even worse: We were almost out of cash. We scraped together our last pennies and came up with a whole $15. That was enough to feed us for three days while we slept on our surf bags on the beach. Our calculations were pretty much on target, but after three days, like it or not, we had to leave. After spending our last 50 cents on a bottle of water, we stood at the side of the road with all our bags and surfboards and stuck out our thumbs. Our mission: Reach the main road 1¾ miles (3 kilometers) away and embark on a hitchhiking adventure. Our goal: the next ATM.

The first car that stopped was driven by a sleazy-looking guy in a shirt who rolled down his window and asked us where were headed.

"TO THE MAIN ROAD."

"FIVE DOLLARS!"

"WE DON'T HAVE ANY MONEY."

Silence. He thought about it.

"HAHAHA, YOU LOSERS!"

And off he went. Fine. That's how things went until finally a white pickup pulled up next to us. The window was slowly lowered. Staring at us was a confidence-inspiring native with a smudgy prison tattoo on his face and a scar above his eye. He suddenly grinned and bared his three teeth, all made of silver.

"TO THE MAIN ROAD? NO PROBLEM. HOP IN."

"GRACIAS!"

So we made it to the main road. Then the guy asked us where exactly we wanted to go. We weren't sure—somewhere to the south. And guess what…he was headed that way too! For the next few hours we lay on our surf bags in the bed of the pickup and enjoyed the balmy air rushing past. Herds of cattle on the road, palm trees, horses pulling carts, a lush green landscape—it all sailed by. It sometimes worried us a little that the guy was driving at lightning speed around poorly maintained switchbacks, especially when he drove full-speed toward a truck that was blasting its horn and its side mirror passed within 1½ feet (0.5 meter) of our heads. Our hair was blown dry, adventure-style. The wild ride continued all the way to Canoa, where our new friend dropped us off right on the beach. Jackpot!

Canoa was another place offering everything the spoiled European heart could desire: ATMs, beer, and a wide variety of foods. We gladly shoveled an enormous helping of fish in seafood curry sauce down our throats.

FISH FILLET WITH SEAFOOD CURRY SAUCE

FAST FOOD

SERVES 2

11 OUNCES (300 G) FROZEN SCALLOPS, SHRIMP, AND SQUID MIX (OR ANY SEAFOOD MIX)

1/2 MEDIUM YELLOW ONION, MINCED

3 TO 5 SPRIGS PARSLEY, LEAVES PLUCKED AND STEMS MINCED

2 CLOVES GARLIC, MINCED

3 TABLESPOONS OLIVE OIL, DIVIDED

1/3 CUP (80 ML) DRY WHITE WINE

2 (5 1/2-OUNCE) (11 OUNCES/300 G TOTAL) WHITE FISH FILLETS, SUCH AS HALIBUT, SOLE, OR COD

SALT

FRESHLY GROUND BLACK PEPPER

1 TEASPOON CURRY POWDER

1/3 CUP (80 ML) HEAVY CREAM

Thaw the seafood in the refrigerator. Braise the onions, parsley stems, and garlic in 1 tablespoon of olive oil. Add the seafood and sauté it for several minutes. Then pour on the white wine. Let the contents of the pan simmer for 5 minutes over low heat.

In a second pan, brown the fish fillets in the remaining 2 tablespoons of olive oil for 4 minutes on each side. Season them with salt and pepper.

Stir the curry powder into the cream and add it to the seafood. Season the seafood curry sauce to taste with salt and pepper and stir in the parsley leaves.

Distribute the fish in shallow bowls and pour the sauce over the top. This dish goes well with pasta, rice, or baked potatoes. And salad. And a nice glass of white wine.

GALÁPAGOS

From Canoa, we rode to Guayaquil, the second-largest city in Ecuador, where you can get a really cheap flight to the Galápagos Islands. We got on a plane and landed on San Cristóbal about two hours later. Once there, we could think of only one word to describe the place: *paradise.*

Everywhere we looked there were wild animals, and almost none of them were afraid of people. When we disembarked from the taxi boat, we had to climb over a herd of surly, half-asleep bull sea lions, who acknowledged us with a few unenthusiastic grunts. To the left, big black lizards watched us from the quay wall. Bright red crabs the size of plates bustled over the rocks on the beach. Several blue-footed boobies and pelicans flew near our heads. It was as though time had stood still. At first glance the small fishing village of Puerto Baquerizo Moreno seemed to be frozen in colonial times.

In the evenings, everyone sat at tables on the same street and chomped on 4-pound (nearly 2 kg) grilled lobsters or fish or pots of mussels, accompanied by cold beer and lots of laughter. We stayed in a small inn for $13 apiece and went surfing at the first sign of daylight, always in the company of a herd of sea lions. They enjoyed splashing around us and surfed a few waves themselves. Below us, we saw sea turtles peacefully plucking algae from the black lava rocks on the bottom. Whenever we temporarily had our fill of waves, we explored the island's interior. There we found an area full of tortoises. These were unbelievably massive prehistoric animals, about 170 years old and weighing 660 pounds (300 kilograms), wheezing like ancient steam engines. Say what?

Galápagos

GORDON
R O C K S

San
Cristóbal

Isla
SANTA
CRUZ

TONGO
Reef

Lobería

There are some damn good surf spots on San Cristóbal. The most difficult and best wave is La Loberia. *Loberia* basically means "sea lion colony" and, like the name says, you share the waves with a herd of sea lions.

Unfortunately, the sea lions aren't the only ones you share the waves with—which is why none of the locals like to surf there. The area around the Galápagos Islands has the world's largest population of sharks. Hammerheads, bull sharks, and tiger sharks are constantly making the rounds. And guess where their favorite hunting ground is? La Loberia, of course. That's what we were told by Raúl, an Ecuadorian surfer I'd met at another surf spot called Tongo Reef. But the wave forecast for La Loberia was so good, we ignored the shark risk and arranged to meet at six o'clock the next morning.

We started out at first light. It was freezing cold and we were dead tired. We were the only people on the beach. Perfect waves. Not a single sea lion in the water—they were all hanging out on the beach. Now, why might that be? We knew very well, but we didn't want to think about it too much. We stood there for half an hour, just staring at the water. Although it was unbelievably clear, the black lava rocks on the bottom made it hard to see below the surface. The combination of clear water and black bottom gave us the creeps. Raúl said:

"NOW YOU KNOW WHAT I MEAN. HERE, YOU ALWAYS HAVE THE FEELING THAT THERE ARE PREDATORS LURKING."

Yeah, I knew exactly what he meant, and my stomach was not happy as I paddled out to a wave. As I sat waiting for

the next set, I felt like I was being served up on a platter. As I sat on the peak and waited, I stole glances at the water, trying to detect any suspicious movement. The first big wave finally came. Raúl was in a somewhat better position, so he took it—an awesome wave—and surfed about 330 feet (100 meters toward the beach. So now I was alone. I stared at the horizon as though I could conjure up a wave through sheer willpower, but the ocean wasn't cooperating. I heard a bubbling in the water behind me and whipped my head around, but I was too late. About 32 feet (10 meters) away I saw a small whirlpool and imagined I could see a dark shadow passing beneath it. The surface was too rough to recognize anything specific, but my imagination filled in the gaps. Although the water was only 57°F (14°C), I suddenly felt hot, like I was sitting in a pot of boiling water. I was totally still, even forgetting to breathe. Again I saw a dark shadow shoot past. This time I was absolutely sure—what the hell!? I

looked anxiously for the next wave but there were none in sight. Suddenly everything went very fast; a black bulky creature shot out of the water right next to me and landed on the surface with a huge splash. A second later, an enormous head surfaced and a bull sea lion sat lazily staring at me. Leaning his head to one side, he started to grunt and bleat. I could have sworn he was laughing at me! He was doing it on purpose! Sure, I was relieved, but I also felt like an idiot. That clown continued paddling around me until a set of waves finally came our way. I took the first one, and as I paddled back to the peak, I saw the sea lion surfing the next wave toward me. A cool dude. We pushed everything else out of our heads and surfed our best session ever until we'd worn ourselves out. Sharks? What sharks?

GALÁPAGOS ISLANDS SURF GUIDE

Here's Raúl, telling us about his favorite spots!

Our new friend Raúl initiated us in the surf secrets of the Galápagos Islands.

I'm Raúl Cabrera, maybe the world's most widely traveled Ecuadorian. I've been all over the world, but I have to say that the Galápagos Islands have the best waves on the planet.

Something about the Galápagos Islands keeps pulling me back. I return here whenever I'm in Ecuador. The first time I surfed here, I was sixteen. There were almost no surfers on the island, so it was too scary to paddle out into the waves alone. Since then everything has changed. Now the Galápagos Islands are our version of Hawaii. My number-one spot here is:

LA LOBERIA −0.92805°N −89.61235°E

It's the most reliable spot in Ecuador, but it's not for the faint-hearted. There's a creepy feeling in the air as soon as you paddle out. You have to pass through a lagoon with sea lions and one or two tiger sharks. The waves are really powerful and as much as 13 feet (4 meters) high. It's a great place for both rights and lefts. On a really good day, you'll find the heaviest drops and the biggest barrels. You'll be shot out of the wave at top speed. It's definitely an adrenaline rush and super training for any surf fan.

My second-favorite spot on San Cristóbal is:

TONGO REEF, −0.90968°N −89.62616°E.

Here you'll have lots of fun with a left point break that's up to 656 feet (200 meters) long. The water is totally clear. You're surrounded by huge sea lions and the locals are extremely friendly. If La Loberia is a little too much for you, you'll find this wave to be a good option because it's always a little smaller. When the La Loberia wave is 10 feet (3 meters) high, Tongo Reef is around 6½ feet (2 meters). But the coolest thing about this place is the animals. If you bring binoculars, you'll see so many different animals it'll blow your mind.

ECUADORIAN SHRIMP CEVICHE

From the Galápagos Islands, we flew back to Guayaquil. Raúl was nice enough to let us stay in his guestroom there. In the evenings, we all went out to eat Ecuadorian ceviche together.

SERVES 4

1 SMALL RED ONION
JUICE OF 2 LIMES OR 1 LEMON
SALT
2¼ POUNDS (1 KG) SMALL SHRIMP, PEELED
AND DEVEINED
1 CUP (240 ML) LIME JUICE
½ CUP (120 ML) ORANGE JUICE
½ CUP KETCHUP
1 TABLESPOON DIJON MUSTARD
1 TABLESPOON SUGAR
1 TOMATO, DICED
FRESHLY GROUND BLACK PEPPER
½ CUP (110 G) YELLOW POPCORN KERNELS
2 TABLESPOONS VEGETABLE OIL, PLUS MORE
FOR SPRINKLING
1 BUNCH CILANTRO, CHOPPED

Peel the onion, halve it, and cut it into thin rings. Soak it in lime or lemon juice for about 30 minutes to take away some of the bite.

Fill a pot half-full with water, sprinkle in a pinch of salt, and bring the water to a boil. Blanch the shrimp in the water for 2 to 3 minutes, until they turn a pink-orange color. Then drain them in a colander, reserving the cooking water.

In a large bowl, combine 1 cup (240 ml) of the shrimp cooking water with the lime juice, the orange juice, ketchup, mustard, and sugar. Then add the shrimp, diced tomato, and onion rings and season with salt and pepper to taste.

Pop the popcorn in the oil in a covered saucepan, following the directions on the package.

Distribute the shrimp among small shallow bowls. Sprinkle with several drops of vegetable oil and the cilantro. Top each of your creations with a small handful of popcorn and serve.

As always, we asked our host to show us the local market. This time Raúl introduced us to another specialty: *bolón*—deep-fried plantains served for breakfast. The plantains are mashed and mixed with sheep's cheese. The market women then shape them into dumplings, press in a handful of crisp bacon and rind pieces, and serve them with a ladleful of meat stock. Extremely filling! After this substantial breakfast, we took a cab to the bus station and embarked on the long overnight journey to Peru.

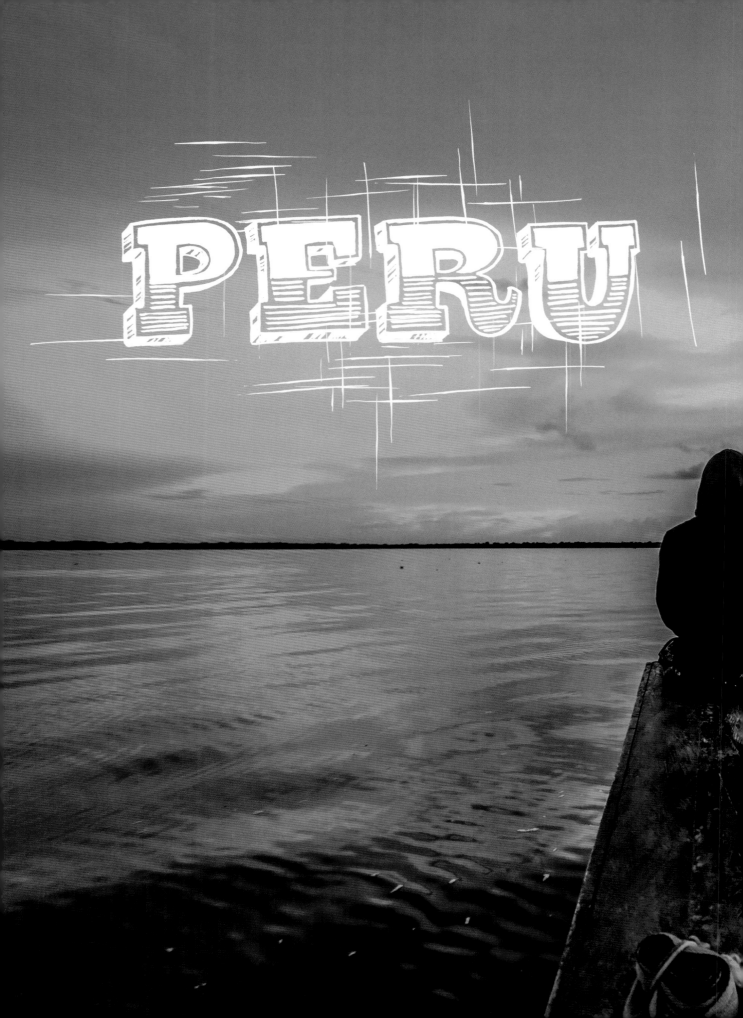

SEE VIDEO:

PERU

IQUITO

MANCORA

Cabo
Blanco
Lobitos

Chicama

Huanchaco

La Herradura

Friends, this is going to be a long chapter. Peru is one huge gold mine, whether it's surfing or food. It's the third-largest country in South America, and the distances are correspondingly long. It has a variety of climate zones, ranging from the tropical Amazonian rain forest to the enormous Atacama Desert in the south to the highland climate of the Andes to the Mediterranean-like feel of the northern coast.

Peruvian cooking is equally diverse and differs according to region. Peru is also where potatoes originally came from and is said to have over 3,900 varieties. Even our hallowed ceviche (for basics, see page 176) came from here, before it spread throughout all of Latin America and, finally, the world. The highlands also have another specialty called *cuy*, roasted guinea pig.

But Peru also has real attractions for surfers, such as the famous wave of Chicama, said to be the longest surfable left in the world. We couldn't wait to explore this country. Even before we left home, it was one of the destinations we were most excited about. And Peru did not disappoint!

233

Machu Picchu

Cusco

Arequipa

Lima

Punta de Bombon

We crossed over the northern border of Peru from Ecuador and had our first stopover in Mancora. Unfortunately, it turned out to be something of a party destination where it's hard to avoid the spring-break vibe. Nevertheless, we found a fantastic market where we were able to buy super-fresh yellowfin tuna. Our Peruvian friend Johana showed us how to transform this tuna into the finest *tiradito con ají amarillo.*

TIRADITO DE ATÚN CON AJÍ AMARILLO

FRESH TUNA WITH PEPPER SAUCE

Ají amarillo is a fruity yellow chile pepper that's extremely common in Peru. It's used in a wide variety of recipes but is also frequently made into a sauce for meat or fish. If you can't find *ají amarillo*, you can use yellow banana chile peppers, which can sometimes be found even in German supermarkets. You can also make the sauce out of regular yellow bell peppers and add half a habanero chile to give it the necessary spiciness, as we've done here.

SERVES 2

AJÍ AMARILLO SAUCE

3 YELLOW BELL PEPPERS, SEEDED AND QUARTERED
SALT
1 HABANERO CHILE (OR LESS FOR LESS SPICINESS)
3 TABLESPOONS VEGETABLE OIL

TIRADITO DE ATÚN

1 1/8 POUNDS (500 G) ULTRA-FRESH TUNA FILLET
1/2 MEDIUM RED ONION
FLEUR DE SEL
JUICE OF 2 LIMES

To make the sauce, remove the seeds from the bell peppers and cut them into quarters. Bring a pot of salted water to a boil and blanch the bell and habanero peppers for 10 minutes. Drain the peppers, let them cool, and then peel them.

Place all of the peppers and the vegetable oil in a blender and purée to make a velvety yellow sauce. Season the sauce with a generous pinch of salt—*et voilà*!

Slice the tuna thinly. Remove the two or three outermost layers from the onion and slice the inner layers into thin rings.

Arrange the tuna slices side by side on a plate and season them with the fleur de sel. Distribute the onion rings over the tuna and drizzle everything with lime juice. Finally, spoon a large dollop of your *ají amarillo* sauce on top. Your *tiradito* is ready.

QUINOA SALAD

Quinoa is also called the "grain of the Incas." The seeds of the quinoa plant are common throughout the Andes and are a favorite salad or side dish, especially in Ecuador, Peru, and Chile. Quinoa is pretty healthy: gluten-free and rich in protein and minerals. And if you dress it right, it tastes great!

SERVES 4

2⅓ CUPS (400 G) QUINOA
2 BAY LEAVES
1 CLOVE GARLIC
1 TABLESPOON UNSALTED BUTTER
4 CREMINI MUSHROOMS, DICED
ZEST AND JUICE FROM 1 LEMON
1 SMALL RED ONION, DICED
1 RED BELL PEPPER, SEEDED AND DICED
1 GREEN BELL PEPPER, SEEDED AND DICED
1 AVOCADO, PITTED, PEELED, AND DICED
½ CUP PITTED KALAMATA OLIVES, FINELY CHOPPED
1 CUP FRESH BASIL LEAVES, TORN INTO PIECES
1 CUP ARUGULA, TORN INTO PIECES
1 CUP FRESH PARSLEY LEAVES, TORN INTO PIECES
½ CUP DARK RAISINS
JUICE OF ½ ORANGE
OLIVE OIL
SALT AND FRESHLY GROUND BLACK PEPPER
¾ CUP (180 ML) CILANTRO SALSA (PAGE 53)

Place the quinoa in a large pot of water and skim off any residue on the surface. Soak the quinoa for 20 minutes. Then pour it through a strainer, return it to the pot, and add water until you have two parts water to one part quinoa. Throw in the bay leaves and garlic and bring the water to a boil. Simmer the quinoa over low heat for about 15 minutes. It's al dente when the germ visibly spirals out around the edges of the grain. Let it stand, covered for 5 minutes. Remove the bay leaves and garlic clove.

Melt the butter in a skillet over medium heat. Sauté the mushrooms in the butter until tender, then add half of the lemon juice to the pan.

Combine the quinoa with the mushrooms, onion, bell peppers, avocado, olives, basil, arugula, parsley, raisins, and orange juice in a large salad bowl. Toss the salad well and add a little olive oil, the rest of the lemon juice, and the lemon zest. Season it with salt and pepper to taste.

Serve the salad in small bowls and top each bowlful with a dollop of the cilantro salsa.

PERU SURF GUIDE

After having met up with our Australian friend and fellow surfer Chris Bailey in Costa Rica, we hooked up with him again, many weeks and 620 miles (thousands of kilometers) later, in northern Peru. Together we traveled down the coast and surfed spots from Mancora to Lima. As an old surfing pro, Chris was nice enough to share his notes on the individual spots. So the following is Chris's personal surf guide:

Peru is a surfer's paradise with an incredible number of waves. From the freezing-cold point breaks in Huanchaco to the super-long left in Chicama, all the way to the warm, sandy barrels of Cabo Blanco—Peru has it all. The window of opportunity for the best swell in the Southern Hemisphere is winter. The swell comes out of the south and is perfect in spots that have lefts. In the summer, there are always swells from the north at spots such as Lobitos and Cabo Blanco. In southern Peru you need a good 3/2 wetsuit, but in the north a rash vest will do.

MANCORA –4.10509˚N –81.05897˚E

Go for a longboard on days when there's not much of swell. Surfing here is best when there's a north or nort west swell and you're not dependent on the tide. You c also rent longboards on the beach by the day!

Mancora is always crowded. The biggest hazard is begi ners turned loose on the wave by irresponsible su instructors. It's a party spot for surfers, so grab a lon board and wash the previous night right out of your boo

CABO BLANCO

LOBITOS

LOBITOS -4.45229°N -81.28570°E

This is one of the best lefts in the area, breaking over slightly rocky sand. Perfect barrels with a southwest swell, which is why it's also fairly crowded. But the vibe is nice and relaxed. The wave itself is crazy. On good days you can surf it for 328 feet (100 meters).

There are two good hostels nearby, right on the bluff. We spent the night at La Casa de Nacho, a friendly little hostel where they showed surfing films every evening and made fantastic pizza. The rooms are cheap and simply furnished and there's a family atmosphere.

CABO BLANCO -4.24974°N -81.23261°E

Cabo Blanco is considered the jewel of South America. The left barrels here could turn out to be the best ride of your life. You enter over flat bedrock and race toward the pier. Definitely not a wave for beginners, because it's a barrel from start to finish! If you really want the best, you need a solid north or northwest swell—preferably with winds from the southwest, but even when the wind blows parallel to the shore, it often doesn't affect the wave.

The city itself offers only the very basics when it comes to accommodations and food. The nearest city worth mentioning is El Alto, which you can reach by mini-van. The prevailing vibe is a sort of local chauvinism,

CHICAMA -7.70517°N -79.45231°E

This famous left is known as the longest wave in the world. It breaks over a sandy bottom and rides are measured in minutes. The wave starts at the farthest tip of the bay. The famous El Hombre section is just to the right of the hostel and is the most fun. This side of the land also gives you a little protection from the south wind.

When the forecast for Huanchaco is good, it's also a good time to visit Chicama. There has to be a solid south/southwest swell to get the high waves, but then they're as high as they come. When the south swell is low, the wave is ideal for beginners because the individual sections don't link up. When the swell is higher, it can get crowded, so just be patient and you'll have your reward.

HUANCHACO -8.08051°N -79.12344°E

Huanchaco is a beach paradise not far from Trujillo. It is THE magnet of the region, with waves that are always a little bit higher than those at Pacaymayo and Chicama. The main wave is a left over a rocky bottom. The surfing is best at mid tide, when the wave can get very long and at some points a little challenging. The section in front of the small pagoda by the Mirador pier is best, although the current running from the north toward the pier makes paddling out treacherous. You might want to wear surf booties. It's generally pretty crowded here, too, but it's well spread out. We can recommend the Surf Hostel Meri.

LIMA −12.17695°N −77.03357°E

Lima isn't exactly known for its waves, but it has a ded-
icated local surfer clique. The main wave breaks in the
sections from Miraflores to Barranco, where fat waves roll
over a sandy bottom. If you're in the city when there's a
south swell, head straight for La Herradura, where you'll
find a left at the south end of the bay. It starts out steep,
then broadens out, and finally ends in a barrel section.
The waves are always breaking so it's always crowded,
although it's worse on weekends.

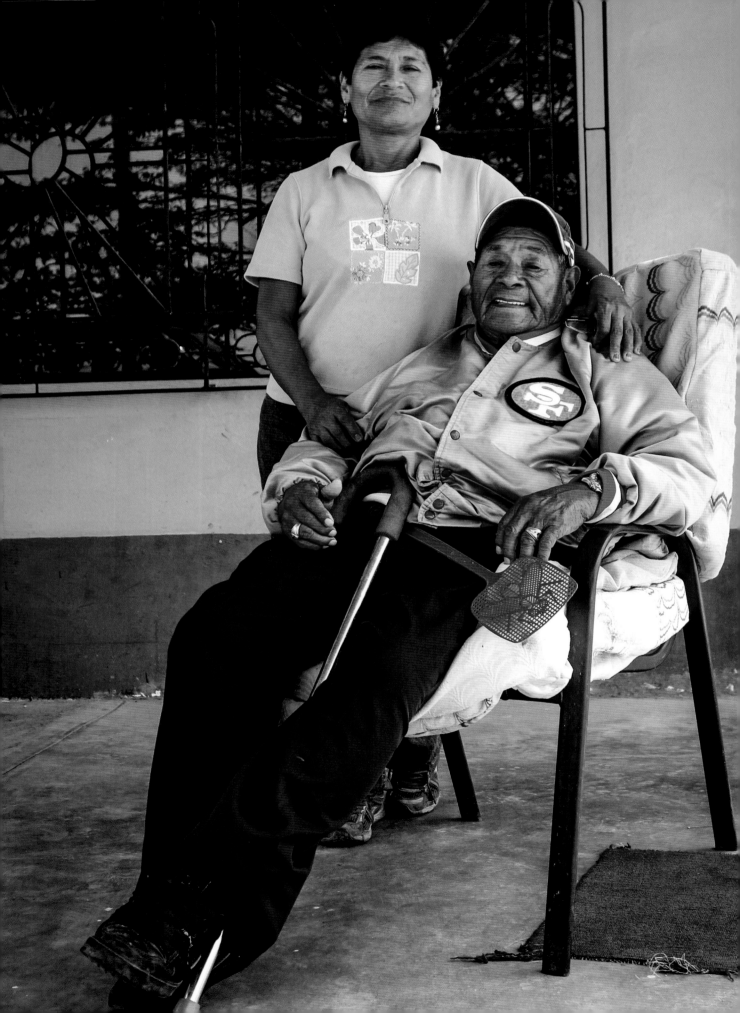

A taxi took us up the dusty gravel road from Chicama to the El Hombre hostel, and as it dropped us off in front of the door, we noticed a very old man eyeing us from his rocking chair. He was wearing skate shoes and a yellowed kepi from the Chicama Surf Contest and had three dogs at his feet. He silently sized us up, then shifted his gaze to the ocean and the waves. The screen door opened and a woman in her late sixties greeted us warmly. She said that her father, El Hombre, no longer liked to talk, but it turned out that she talked enough for both of them. She told us El Hombre was the first person ever to surf Chicamas, talked about the latest good swells, and related various stories from her life. She also informed us that her brother, who worked in the hostel, was having a birthday the next day. As a pre-birthday celebration, we shopped and made *causa* for the entire crew. It tasted so good that even El Hombre thawed a little. In a burst of chattiness, he actually asked us if Hitler was still alive. A real wiseguy.

CAUSA CRIOLLA
CHICKEN, POTATO, AND VEGETABLE TORTE

A sort of torte with layers of mashed potatoes, chicken, avocado, and salsa, this can also have other fillings, but we think these taste best. It's unbelievably delicious, as well as a feast for the eyes. The torte is generally eaten lukewarm or cold. You need either four 6-inch (15 cm) diameter ring molds or one big 9-inch (23 cm) springform pan, in which case you'll be making one huge torte.

SERVES 4

CHICKEN
4 LARGE CHICKEN LEG QUARTERS, PREFERABLY ORGANIC
3 TABLESPOONS OLIVE OIL
2 TEASPOONS WHOLE BLACK PEPPERCORNS
SEA SALT
2 TEASPOONS SWEET PAPRIKA
4 CLOVES GARLIC

MASHED POTATOES
5 POUNDS (2.3 KG) RUSSET POTATOES
SALT
AJÍ AMARILLO SAUCE (PAGE 262)

REMAINING FILLING
1 TABLESPOON UNSALTED BUTTER
2 TABLESPOONS DARK RAISINS
1 BUNCH CILANTRO, CHOPPED
1 BUNCH MINT, CHOPPED
3 LIMES
2 AVOCADOS
1 SMALL RED ONION
1 MEDIUM-LARGE CHILE PEPPER
½ CUP PITTED KALAMATA OLIVES

Preheat the oven to 430°F (220°C). Rinse the chicken leg quarters thoroughly and pat them dry with paper towels. Place the chicken on a roasting rack set in a roasting pan or casserole dish and drizzle it with a decent amount of olive oil. Crush the peppercorns in a mortar and pestle and mix them with the salt and paprika. Rub the chicken well with these seasonings.

Crush the unpeeled garlic cloves with the blade of a chef's knife and add them to the roasting pan. Using the top third of the oven, roast the chicken for at least 1 hour, turning it once after 40 minutes and stirring everything well. Once the skin has formed bubbles and becomes crispy and brown, the meat will practically fall off the bones.

While the chicken is roasting, make the mashed potatoes. Place a large pot of water on the stove, add a large pinch of salt, and bring the water to a boil. Peel the potatoes and boil them until you can easily pierce them with a fork. Depending on the size of the potatoes, this could take 25 to 35 minutes. Drain the potatoes and let them cool slightly. Mash them coarsely in the pot using a potato masher.

By now, your chicken should be done. Remove the roasting pan from the oven and let it cool on the stove. Add 5 generous tablespoons of the melted chicken-fat marinade from the bottom of the roasting pan to the mashed potatoes. This gives them an awesome flavor. Then add the *ají amarillo* sauce to the potatoes and mash them well, but leaving some chunks. You're going to build an actual potato tower, so they have to be firm. Now you've got your foundation.

Next, bone the cooled chicken with a fork and chop it coarsely. Melt the butter in a large skillet over low heat. As soon as it starts to foam, take the garlic cloves out of the roasting pan and crush them with a knife blade, thus squeezing the buttery garlic paste out of the peel. Add the garlic to the pan. Add the chopped chicken and toss it in the garlic butter.

Stir the raisins, cilantro, and mint (reserving some of both for garnish) into the chicken and squeeze the limes over the pan. Remove the chicken from the heat and set it aside.

Peel the avocados, remove the pits, and cut the flesh into strips. Peel the red onion. Heads up, here's a secret Peruvian trick that we've mentioned several times in this book already. To make the raw onion taste a little milder, remove the two or three thick, outer layers from the onion. The inner layers are much milder and sweeter than the outer ones. Chop this "onion heart" coarsely.

Remove the seeds from the chile pepper and chop half of it finely (the other half will serve as garnish). Combine the avocado, onions, and chopped chile pepper.

Now it's time to build your potato towers. Place the ring molds (or springform pan) on plates and fill each ring with a layer of mashed potatoes ¾ to 1⅛ inches (2 to 3 cm) thick. Smooth out the top. Next add a layer of the avocado-onion-chile mixture. And then comes the best part: a thick layer of the chicken mixture. By now, your first guests will be arriving; they'll be drawn to the kitchen by the fragrance, and they'll want a taste. Don't let them have a single bite! Since you're the one doing all the work, they can just wait.

For the roof, top your towers with a ⅓-inch-thick (1 cm) layer of mashed potatoes. Garnish each torte with the remaining chopped herbs, a pinch of paprika, red chile strips, and some Kalamata olives. And that's it. Now you can feed the ravenous wolves by serving right out of the molds. *Provecho!*

From Chicama, we caught a bus to Lima, where we hooked up with our friend Luka, who does corporate designs for Lima's best restaurants. He was the ideal guide for our culinary treasure hunt. We struck gold: We had the world's best ceviche, octopus in a purple olive sauce, grilled scallops, sea urchin *tiradito*, smoked and dried tuna, beef heart skewers, razor clams, quinoa salad, mountains of incredibly delicious roast pork sandwiches with mint sauce and sliced sweet potatoes, a sort of mashed potato-chicken layered torte called Causa Criolla (page 246), beef tripe soup, larded leg of lamb, Chinese-Peruvian fried rice...the list could go on for hours. Peruvian cuisine should really be declared a UNESCO World Heritage treasure. It's unbelievable that it's not better known in Europe. But we're going to change that right now with our best Peruvian recipes! Fortunately, Lima also has several nice surf spots, otherwise everyone here would be totally overweight. Ourselves included.

Meanwhile, we were ready for more tattoos. Searching online, we found out about a fantastic Brazilian tattoo artist named Tania Maia who was working in Lima. We made an appointment on the spot! I added three tattoos: an eagle ray, a cuckoo, and the Spanish phrase *EL MAR, MI ALMA* ("the ocean, my soul"). Cozy added a lime squeezer to the collection of kitchen appliances on his leg. Tania was awesome. She did the most incredibly exact and detailed dot and line work tattoos. Fortunately,

she was also willing to draw some illustrations for this book! Check out pages 11, 12, and 122.

At the end of our culinary adventure in Lima, we hosted a big dinner party for our new friends. It was our first time preparing all the recipes we'd just learned.

BASIC CEVICHE

We already told you about classic ceviche, which is native to Peru, on page 176. According to the best ceviche maker in the world, you need exactly five ingredients for perfect ceviche: fillet of sole, limes, red onion, salt, and pepper.

SERVES 2

1 MEDIUM RED ONION
1 (5¾-OUNCE) SUSHI-QUALITY SOLE FILLET, WELL CHILLED
JUICE OF 3 TO 5 LIMES
SEA SALT, PREFERABLY FLEUR DE SEL
FRESHLY GROUND BLACK PEPPER

Remove the two or three outermost layers from the onion. The inner layers are milder, providing a fine onion flavor without stinging your eyes. Halve the onion and cut it into thin strips.

Cut the sole fillet into ⅓ by ¾-inch (1 by 2-cm) pieces. Place the fish and onions in a bowl and add the lime juice, salt, and pepper. You'll have to rely on your own taste to achieve the correct balance between lime, fish, and seasonings.

Exact amounts are impossible to give because every lime differs in terms of its ripeness and, therefore, its degree of sourness. Onions come in different sizes, as do sole fillets. Just start with a small amount and gradually experiment until you've met your own personal flavor expectations.

As a side dish, Peruvians serve cold sweet potatoes cooked until tender and mild Peruvian corn. You can order the corn online, but we've never tried it ourselves. Or you can roast standard European canned corn in a pan and salt it well. In *cevicherías*, this side dish is often served as a snack.

Working off this basic ceviche recipe, you can experiment with a wide variety of interesting flavor combinations. You'll find several of our favorite versions on the next few pages.

OCTOPUS CEVICHE

For octopus ceviche, even the ceviche chef makes an exception, because octopus can't be eaten raw. Simmering it for an hour in a little stock will make it tender and juicy.

SERVES 4

2 STALKS CELERY, COARSELY CHOPPED, PLUS 2 WHOLE STALKS
1 CARROT, PEELED AND COARSELY CHOPPED
1 MEDIUM YELLOW ONION, COARSELY CHOPPED
8 TO 10 SPRIGS PARSLEY, CHOPPED
2 BAY LEAVES
1 (2¼– TO 3⅓–POUND/1 TO 1.5 KG) CLEANED OCTOPUS
1 MEDIUM RED ONION
JUICE OF 4 LIMES
1 RED FRESNO CHILE PEPPER, SEEDED AND MINCED
1 BUNCH MINT, MINCED
SEA SALT AND FRESHLY GROUND BLACK PEPPER

Bring a large pot of water to a boil and add the chopped celery, carrot, yellow onion, parsley, bay leaves, and octopus. There should be enough water to cover everything. If not, add a little more. Simmer the octopus for 1 hour, then remove it from the water and let it cool. Discard the water and its contents.

Remove the two or three outermost layers from the red onion and cut the inner layers into fine strips. Cut the remaining 2 stalks of celery lengthwise into quarters, and then into paper-thin slices.

Cut the octopus into bite-size pieces and place it in a bowl with the red onion and sliced celery. Toss with the lime juice, chile, and mint. Season with salt and pepper to taste.

FILLET OF SOLE CEVICHE WITH PAPAYA AND POMEGRANATE

The rule with ceviche is that it generally goes well with anything sour. But we prefer to experiment with combinations involving sweet fruits. It makes the ceviche especially flavorful and refreshing. In the summer, there's nothing better!

SERVES 2

½ MEDIUM RED ONION
½ PAPAYA
1⅛ POUNDS (500 G) SUSHI-QUALITY SOLE FILLETS
½ RED FRESNO CHILE PEPPER, SEEDED AND MINCED
1 BUNCH CILANTRO, CHOPPED
SEEDS FROM ½ POMEGRANATE
JUICE FROM 3 LIMES
SEA SALT AND FRESHLY GROUND BLACK PEPPER

Remove the two or three outermost layers from the onion and cut the inner layers into thin strips. Peel the papaya and cut the flesh into ⅓-inch (1 cm) cubes. Cut the sole fillet into ⅓-inch (1 cm) cubes.

Mix all of the ingredients together in a bowl, seasoning with salt and pepper to taste. Dig in!

TROUT CEVICHE WITH CANTALOUPE AND STAR FRUIT

SERVES 2

1 TABLESPOON BLACK SESAME SEEDS
½ MEDIUM RED ONION
1½ CANTALOUPE OR HONEYDEW MELON
1 STAR FRUIT
1⅛ POUNDS (500 G) SUSHI-QUALITY
BROOK TROUT FILLETS
1 SCALLION, THINLY SLICED
1 BUNCH CILANTRO, CHOPPED
JUICE OF 4 LIMES

Briefly toast the sesame seeds in a small dry skillet over low heat. Remove the two or three outermost layers from the onion and cut the inner layers into thin strips. Peel the melon and slice it finely. Quarter the star fruit and slice it thinly. Cut the trout fillet into ⅓ by ¾-inch (1 by 2-cm) pieces.

Mix all of the ingredients except for the sesame seeds in a bowl, setting aside a little of the cilantro and star fruit for garnish. Then sprinkle the sesame seeds over the top.

Serve the ceviche on plates—unless you all decide to eat it directly out of the bowl. Garnish with cilantro and star fruit.

SALMON CEVICHE WITH GRANNY SMITH APPLE AND COCONUT MILK

FAST FOOD

SERVES 2

- ½ MEDIUM RED ONION
- ½ GRANNY SMITH APPLE
- 1⅓ POUNDS (500 G) SUSHI-QUALITY SALMON FILLETS
- 1 BUNCH CILANTRO, CHOPPED
- ¾ CUP (180 ML) UNSWEETENED COCONUT MILK
- JUICE OF 4 TO 6 LIMES
- SEA SALT AND FRESHLY GROUND BLACK PEPPER
- TOASTED BAGUETTE SLICES, FOR SERVING

Remove the two or three outermost layers from the onion and cut the inner layers into thin strips. Cut the apple into eighths, and then into thin strips. Cut the salmon into thin strips.

Mix all of the ingredients except for the baguette together, seasoning with salt and pepper to taste. Eat the ceviche right out of the bowl, or distribute it among plates, and serve it with the baguette slices.

CONCHAS A LA PARRILLA

CONCHAS A LA PARRILLA

GRILLED SCALLOPS IN A WHITE WINE–WORCESTERSHIRE SAUCE

These grilled scallops are the best. Our friend Luka showed us how he prepares them with a tangy white wine–Worcestershire sauce and then tops them with Parmesan. Say no more.

SERVES 8 AS AN APPETIZER

1 CLOVE GARLIC, MINCED

1 BUNCH CILANTRO, MINCED

5 OUNCES DRY WHITE WINE

2 TABLESPOONS WORCESTERSHIRE SAUCE

JUICE OF 1 LIME

8 MEDIUM SCALLOPS IN THE SHELLS

1 CUP (100 G) GRATED PARMESAN

SEA SALT AND FRESHLY GROUND BLACK PEPPER

Fire up the grill to medium-high.

In a small bowl, combine the garlic, cilantro, white wine, Worcestershire sauce, and lime juice to make the sauce.

Lay the scallops in their shells side by side on the grill. Pour 1 to 2 tablespoons of the sauce onto each scallop and grill them for 2½ to 3½ minutes per side.

Remove the scallops from the grill, keeping them in their shells, and sprinkle the cheese over the top. Season them with salt and pepper to taste, let them cool briefly, and serve.

PULPO AL OLIVO
OCTOPUS WITH OLIVES

This dish is one of our all-time top five Peruvian dishes. It's unique and spectacular, in terms of both color and flavor. In Peru, the olive sauce is made with Botija olives. These are large olives with purple flesh. When puréed, they become a bright purple cream that's served over the octopus, a real eye-catcher. It's rare to find Botija olives in Germany, but Kalamata olives have a similar flavor. We've tried it—it doesn't look as spectacular, but the flavor is virtually the same.

SERVES 4

1 (2¼- TO 3⅓-POUND/1 TO 1.5 KG) CLEANED OCTOPUS
2 LARGE EGG YOLKS
1 CLOVE GARLIC, PEELED
1 TEASPOON YELLOW MUSTARD
JUICE OF 2 LIMES
1 CUP (240 ML) EXTRA-VIRGIN OLIVE OIL
ABOUT 20 PITTED BLACK OLIVES (SUCH AS KALAMATA, OR ANY FAT, FLESHY VARIETY)
½ MEDIUM RED ONION
1 HEART OF ROMAINE LETTUCE
2 TABLESPOONS CHOPPED FRESH PARSLEY
TOASTED BAGUETTE SLICES, FOR SERVING

Bring a large pot of water to a simmer and simmer the octopus for 1 hour, making sure it is always completely covered with liquid. Then remove it from the pot and let it cool.

Combine the egg yolks, garlic clove, mustard, and half of the lime juice in a blender and purée. With the blender running on the lowest setting, gradually add the olive oil in a thin stream until you have a mayonnaise. Then add the olives and purée again to make a smooth cream.

Remove the two or three outermost layers from the onion and cut the inner layers into thin strips. Cut the lettuce and cut into thin strips.

Cut the octopus arms into rings and the body into bite-size strips. Combine the octopus pieces with the onion, parsley, and the remaining lime juice. Arrange the lettuce on a plate, distribute the octopus on top, and drizzle the olive dressing over everything. Arrange the toasted baguette slices around the edges of the plate and enjoy!

WELCOME TO THE JUNGLE!

In Lima we met up with our friend Jana, who joined us for a month on our trip through Peru. First the three of us flew to Iquitos, a city in the middle of the Peruvian Amazon rain forest. There are no roads to this city of over 400,000. You can reach it only by flying or traveling five days by boat—it's way, way off the beaten track. To save time, we decided to fly. Not a bad idea, as it turned out, because the airplane window was the perfect place from which to view the thousands of small and large rivers snaking through the jungle on their way to the Amazon River. We felt like little kids, about to set out on an adventure that was just waiting for us.

Soon afterward, we were walking along the promenade beside the Amazon and observing the locals going about their daily business, living in simple wooden huts directly on the shore. The huts were built in such a way that

months, they would simply float. Next to one of these huts was a small boat with a bamboo roof. We wanted to scout around a little—so why not just knock? We made our way across a decrepit plank no wider than a curbstone. At the hut we were welcomed with open arms by a broadly grinning Peruvian man in his late thirties. Giving us all hugs, he led us through the hut to the floating terrace where his boat was docked. Some kittens were playing in a box and two pigs were grunting in a tiny enclosure. A woman was making soup over an open fire and the scent of fresh fish was in the air. Our new friend's name was Edwin, and he'd been taking visitors out on his boat to see the Amazonian sights for ten years. He was extremely happy that we'd come to him. He didn't speak English, so he was seldom able to give tours to foreigners. Fortunately for us, after almost ten months of traveling around Latin America we

We explained to Edwin that we wanted to go for a short ride without a lot of structure, our main goal being to enjoy the sunset. Edwin and a boy who'd so far been sitting silently in the boat immediately started up the outboard motor, and off we went. The boy steered the boat while Edwin sat with us in the bow and told us how grateful he was that we'd come to him and not to one of the many agencies where most tourists paid tons of money for organized jungle tours. Apparently most of the dollars went to the three largest providers and only a little wound up in the pockets of individuals. We, however, were chugging down the Amazon with Edwin at a leisurely pace, sitting in the bow and enjoying the balmy breeze. Actually, what we really would have liked was for Edwin to take us deeper into the rain forest, where we could spend a few days away from everything the standard tourist came to see in the Amazon region. Maybe visit some remote village, do something that felt "authentic" and not a mass-produced tourist package. When we said this to Edwin, he thought about it for a moment, then nodded and told us about a tiny village in the rain forest where friends of his lived in a hut on the banks of a branch of the Amazon. It was about a five-hour journey by

boat and he was sure we could spend the night there. Our faces lit up and we all said, Let's do it! The only thing was, how much was it going to cost? We prepared ourselves for a huge dollar amount, having in the back of our minds the prices that agencies charged for a "cool two-day jungle tour," including a chance to hold a tarantula—around $180 a piece. What would Edwin charge if we booked his boat for us alone for a multiday tour? It was sure to be horrific, and we would never be able to afford it! It turned out that our estimates were completely off base. Edwin wanted a mere $50 per person for the entire tour, including fuel. Really? Then it's a deal!

We'd just been thinking that it couldn't get any better when the Amazon gave us yet another gift: River dolphins appeared around the boat and swam beside us for a while as we watched the sun go down behind the silhouette of the thousands of wooden huts on shore. If there's such a thing as a perfect moment, this was it. We then bought spicy *anticuchos* from a stand, sat on the quay wall, and enjoyed the quiet.

ANTICUCHOS CON AJÍ AMARILLO

BEEF HEARTS WITH YELLOW BELL PEPPER SAUCE

These spicy-hot beef heart skewers are one of Peru's most common street-food specialties. They're usually served with potatoes and *ají amarillo* sauce. They're best when cooked over a hot grill, but a pan works just as well.

SERVES 4

MARINADE

- 1 CLOVE GARLIC, MINCED
- 2 TABLESPOONS RED CHILI PASTE
- 3 TABLESPOONS RED WINE VINEGAR
- 3 TABLESPOONS OLIVE OIL
- 1 TABLESPOON DRIED OREGANO
- 1 TEASPOON GROUND CUMIN

2¼ POUNDS (1 KG) BEEF HEART, SLICED INTO STRIPS

AMARILLO SAUCE

- SEA SALT
- 3 YELLOW BELL PEPPERS
- ½ HABANERO CHILE
- 3 TABLESPOONS OLIVE OIL
- 1 SHALLOT

POTATOES

- 1⅔ POUNDS RUSSET POTATOES
- ⅔ POUND SWEET POTATOES
- SALT
- VEGETABLE OIL, FOR FRYING
- FRESHLY GROUND BLACK PEPPER

For the marinade, mix together all of the ingredients to make a spicy paste. Rub the meat pieces with a thick layer of this paste and thread them onto 8 skewers. Cover the skewers and set them aside.

To make the sauce, bring a pot of salted water to a boil. Remove the seeds from the bell peppers, and cut them into quarters. Blanch the bell pepper pieces and the habanero for 10 minutes in the boiling water. Drain the peppers, and as soon as the pepper quarters are cool enough, peel them. Combine the bell peppers and habanero in a blender and purée them with the olive oil until smooth. Peel the shallot, dice it finely, and add it to the peppers. Season the sauce with salt to taste. Set aside.

Clean the russet potatoes and sweet potatoes. Bring another pot of salted water to a boil and cook the potatoes. Depending on the size of the potatoes, this could take 25 to 35 minutes. About 10 minutes after you place the russet potatoes in the water, add the sweet potatoes, since they have a shorter cooking time. The potatoes are done when you can pierce them easily with a knife. Pour off the water and set the potatoes aside.

Heat a little oil on a large griddle over medium-high heat and sear the skewers for 3 minutes on each side. They'll taste even better on the grill! Don't forget to season them with salt and pepper.

Cut the potatoes into thick slices and arrange them on plates with 2 skewers each. Top it all off with a heaping spoonful of the *ají amarillo* sauce. Now you can enjoy Peru's most popular street-food dish!

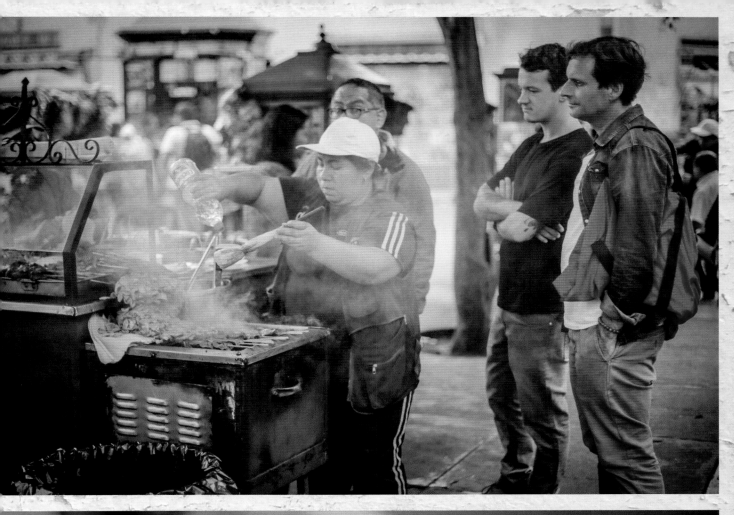

The following day, we set out at first light in Edwin's boat. Our first stop was the Belen Market, a giant corrugated-metal slum that floods in winter and has large areas that can only be reached by boat. We stepped on shore and slogged through the mud to the nearest stands. The smell was, let's just say—funky. All around us was complete chaos. Drunken homeless people staggered along the narrow muddy paths looking for a small patch to sleep on. There were street-food shacks every 10 feet (3 meters) and the foods they were selling were beyond description—but we'll give it a try anyway. Turtle soup simmered in a turtle shell over an open fire. Another stand was selling grilled armored catfish that looked like a cross between a dragon and a prehistoric fish. I'd seen these fish before in an aquarium. If I'd known they were edible, maybe I would have already tried one. There were small mounds of cooked turtle eyes for the tasting. A man was filleting an alligator. There were little *jugueterías* where they made refreshing smoothies out of the many jungle fruits. Whole goat legs were simmering in giant, dented-up kettles. We bought as many different foods as we could carry—our breakfast to go—and continued on through the mud. The market stands were bending under the weight of their wares. Our eyes nearly popped out of our heads at the sight of all those exotic fruits, most of which we'd never seen before. We bought a handful of each to sample. There was every kind of flavor, from sweet to bitter to sour to fermented.

The market's "medical district" offered every kind of miracle remedy imaginable. Shrunken monkey heads were displayed next to snake skeletons and alligator feet. We saw thousands of bottles of unknown liquids in every color of the rainbow, powders, bunches of dried medicinal herbs, and various pastes. One plastic bottle containing a reddish brown liquid was labeled "Sangre de (something-or-other)," meaning some sort of blood. I asked the woman looking like a witch at the stand from whom or from what had she taken the blood. She just laughed and explained that it was only the juice of a jungle tree. Very reassuring.

Although we could have spent days in this market, Edwin urged us to get going. The Amazon was calling! Not wanting to arrive at the home of our rain forest hosts empty-handed, we bought little presents: soap, rice, and candy for the kids. Then we scrambled back onto the boat and shoved off. Once we were on the water, we eagerly unpacked our market purchases and sampled them all. It was quite a feast.

The boat tour was incredibly relaxing. Edwin had installed hammocks beneath the bamboo roof, which is where we spent most of the trip, while Jana sat in the bow enjoying the breeze. We saw countless boats, ships, and dugouts go by, people washing their clothes in the river, fishermen raising their nets, kids waving at us from shore. It was idyllic. The Amazon gently rocked us to sleep, and when Edwin woke us up a few hours later, we

were already there. We packed up our stuff and jumped on shore. Riding in a strange sort of moped-pickup, we followed a small path through the rain forest to our destination. What we found when we got there exceeded all our expectations. Two small wooden huts with palm branch roofs built on wooden stilts and joined by a little bridge stood directly on the shore of a small branch of the Amazon. The thick jungle started just behind them. A horde of kids were paddling around in the river when we arrived, but as soon they spotted us, they charged straight at us, yelling and jumping around. A tiny grandmother watched us from a window. We climbed the ladder to the huts and Edwin introduced everybody. We looked around the simple shelter: One hut was divided into a bedroom and a living room. In one corner was a bathtub that was currently occupied by the family pet: a baby alligator. What else? There was a bridge to the second hut, which functioned as an eat-in kitchen. The remains of several logs were smoldering in a homemade stove. There was no electricity, no toilets—no doubt about it, we were in the jungle. First we had a swim in the small brownish-colored branch of the Amazon that flowed past the huts. Edwin told us that the river was full of piranhas, but we shouldn't be afraid because piranhas were practically blind and were attracted only by the scent of meat or blood in the

water. That's why they didn't bite swimmers. Unless, of course, you had a big open wound. In that case, stay out of the water.

Then came the cooking. To celebrate our arrival, one of the family's three chickens that were currently pecking at worms in the grass under the hut was going to have to bite the dust. The five-year-old son chased it around and around until he finally caught it by the tail. Then he passed it to the lady of the hut, who grabbed it by the neck and swung it in a circle just once. Crack, neck broken, dead. The chicken kept on flapping its wings for a few seconds and then stopped. I started plucking the chicken. It was my first time, and it was really weird. The body was still warm—that just didn't feel right. As a city kid, I knew chickens either as cold and featherless, or as already fried. But that's why I was there, to have new experiences. Minutes later, the whole hen went into the pot. The *señora* prepared a simple chicken soup with rice and cilantro. She told us that one of her children was sick and this soup was an effective remedy for tropical diarrhea. Eat this soup for two days, and you'll be good as new. Since it's not unusual for travelers abroad to suffer this nasty tropical ailment, here's the recipe.

JUNGLE CHICKEN SOUP

SERVES 10

1 (3¾-POUND) WHOLE CHICKEN, PREFERABLY ORGANIC

2⅓ CUPS (400 G) WHITE RICE

2 STALKS CELERY, COARSELY CHOPPED

1 CARROT, PEELED AND COARSELY CHOPPED

1 MEDIUM YELLOW ONION, COARSELY CHOPPED

1 BUNCH CILANTRO

8 TO 10 SPRIGS PARSLEY, CHOPPED

1 BAY LEAF

SALT

LIME JUICE

Place the chicken in a large pot and add just enough water to cover it. Bring the water to a boil, add the rice, celery, carrot, onion, cilantro, parsley, and bay leaf, and simmer for 1½ hours.

Remove the chicken from the pot, let cool slightly, and pull the meat off the bones, cleaning the bones very well. Add the chicken meat back to the pot and season the soup with salt and lime juice to taste. (It shouldn't be too spicy, because that would be hard on the digestive tract.)

Feel better soon!

SLOW FOOD

It was now 6:30, the sun had gone down, and it was rapidly getting dark. The family made room in the kitchen and prepared our beds: two mattresses with mosquito netting draped over them like a small tent. We weren't expecting so much luxury; we'd already prepared ourselves for a night on hard bamboo cots. We lay on our backs and listened to the jungle. There were so many sounds we'd never heard before. It rustled and chirped and howled and twittered—background audio that was much more effective at putting us to sleep than any commercial white-noise CD. Unfortunately, every once in a while one of the remaining chickens would wander through the kitchen, clucking and making noise. It was probably looking for its missing comrade. How did it get up here, anyway? Chickens can't fly, can they?

At dawn the hut came alive. Someone must have gone fishing the night before, because there were already fresh, fragrant, freshwater fish in the kitchen. The oldest daughter—I'd guess she was around twelve—started scaling, cutting open, and gutting the fish with expert movements. Without hesitation, I unwrapped our kitchen knife and joined in. The whole family eyed me skeptically, watching my every move. Although I'd caught and cleaned my first fish when I was eight years old, being watched like that made me feel like it was my first time. I added my first cleaned fish to the girl's pile. She smiled triumphantly, picked it up again, and removed the inner gills with the tip of a knife. Shit, I'd forgotten out of stage fright. Touché. These people were very proud of their traditional culinary skills. Still, I must have done all right because she handed me the next fish. A little while later, we were eating fish soup with boiled yucca root. This yucca, by the way, is in no way related to the potted yucca plant in your living room. It's the root of a bouquet-like tree that's found throughout Latin America. In Germany we know it as tapioca or manioc. It tastes mildly potato-like.

After our stomachs were fed, Jana, Cozy, and I, plus Edwin and the silent helmsman, climbed into the family's little wooden boat for a scouting expedition deeper into the jungle. One of the family's sons also came along and brought his slingshot. The narrow green river was hemmed in by jungle on both sides. As we left one branch of the river and entered another, the water suddenly turned an entirely different color. Whereas one branch was dark brown, the water in the other branch was emerald green. Thousands of colorful birds sat on tree branches, complaining about the uninvited guests. Herons dove for fish. A curious falcon rose gracefully into the air and floated above our boat for a while. Fish snapped at flies. Slightly oversized butterflies fluttered from shore to shore—at first we thought they were some sort of strange, colorful bats. Edwin laughed at us, but otherwise nobody said a word because there was just so much to see. Finally Edwin switched off the motor and steered the boat alongside a fallen tree that was lying in the river. Water lilies formed a thick carpet all around its branches. Edwin declared that this was the perfect spot to fish for piranhas. He handed each of us a wooden rod with a meter of fishing line attached and a hook on the end. Fishing, jungle-style. Edwin unwrapped half a fish that he'd pilfered before breakfast and skillfully cut it into small pieces for bait. Cozy dragged the first piece of bait through the water next to the boat, felt a tug on the line, and pulled the hook out of the water—the bait was gone. Then, the next piece of bait. After a few seconds, Cody felt another tug on the line and whipped it out of the water. A fat, shiny, silvery-orange-colored fish whizzed through the air thrashing at hyper-warp speed and, at the last moment, jumped off the hook and disappeared. This continued for 20 frustrating minutes, until we'd used up all the bait. Silent and disappointed, we set off for more. But the Amazon was on our side after all. The boy steering the boat, who so far hadn't said a word, suddenly jumped up and yelled something at Edwin in pidgin Spanish. We steered toward a bundle of feathers floating in the water—it was a dead river seagull. Edwin pulled it out of the river and chopped it into bite-size pieces of seagull meat that would be absolutely irresistible to piranhas. Even better, he told us, seagull meat was much tougher than fish and wouldn't come off the hook so easily.

The next time we came to a downed tree, we stopped and tried again. And it really did work! There was a tug on the line, Cozy whipped it out of the water, and a piranha sailed straight into the boat. Great! We carefully removed the hook. The fish's teeth were razor-sharp and it was snapping them every which way, making strange clicking noises. We examined it closely: Its belly was an unbelievably intense and shimmering shade of orange while the rest of its body was bright silver, studded with dark spots. It was still young, barely 6 inches (15 centimeters). Our hunting instincts were aroused. We chucked our prey into a bucket of water, baited our hooks with more seagull, and cast out our lines. Now we were catching fish hand over fist. On the left side of the boat I caught a sardine (apparently they like seagull, too), and on the right side, Cozy brought up another piranha. The bucket filled up rapidly and the seagull, like the day, was eventually spent. Satisfied, we made our way back to our family.

PIRANHAS

You won't find piranhas at European latitudes. But in the Amazon region of Peru, they're a highly sustainable, abundant source of food that's easy to catch. Since piranhas don't really have a distinct flavor, you can substitute local freshwater fish. Ask your fishmonger for a recommendation.

SERVES 2

1 EAR CORN, SHUCKED
4 (1-POUND) FRESHWATER FISH, CLEANED
ALL-PURPOSE FLOUR, FOR BREADING
SALT AND FRESHLY GROUND BLACK PEPPER
VEGETABLE OIL, FOR FRYING
1 CLOVE GARLIC, CRUSHED
½ MEDIUM RED ONION, SLICED INTO THIN RINGS
1 TOMATO, DICED
3 TABLESPOONS RED WINE VINEGAR OR HERB-FLAVORED VINEGAR
2 DASHES TABASCO SAUCE
½ CUP PITTED KALAMATA OLIVES
1 HARD-BOILED EGG
2 TABLESPOONS UNSALTED BUTTER
2 SPRIGS PARSLEY, TORN INTO PIECES

Cut the ear of corn in half crosswise. Bring a pot of water to a boil and simmer the corn for 8 to 10 minutes. Then remove it from the water and let it cool.

Preheat the oven to 150°F (70°C), or the lowest setting possible. Rinse the fish and pat it dry. In a shallow bowl, season the flour with salt and pepper. Dredge the fish in this mixture on both sides. Heat some oil in a skillet over medium heat, and fry the fish for 2 minutes on each side, until the breading is nice and brown. Take the fish out of the pan, place on a baking sheet, and keep it warm in the oven.

Once again, heat a little oil in the skillet, and add the garlic, onion, and tomato. Sauté briefly over medium-low heat, then add the vinegar, Tabasco, and olives and stir to combine.

Peel and halve the egg. Arrange the fish on plates and pour the sauce over the top. Place half an egg and half an ear of corn next to the fish and top the corn with a pat of butter. Sprinkle some parsley over the top, season with salt and pepper to taste, and eat.

As we motored along the Amazon, the boy who'd been so quiet up until now shyly joined us in the bow. He took a deep breath and introduced himself: His name was Segundo, he was seventeen years old, and he wanted to tell us his story. We were intrigued. All this time he hadn't said a word, which made what he now had to say even more profound. He told his story with so much emotion, we could see his scars and tattoos—we think it wouldn't be inappropriate to include it here.

He was born in a small, decrepit shack at Belen Market. His mother was an alcoholic and his father did nothing to support the family. When he was twelve years old, he ran away from home. He smoked his first pot, and started drinking and sniffing gasoline. He stole his first purse when he was thirteen. He described how scared he was at first and how he got over it with time. He was in his first knife fight at fourteen. He was sleeping under a table in the market, already a lost soul. He would have liked to have gone home, but his mother didn't want anything more to do with him. So all he had left was his high and the street.

Segundo was silent for a moment, stroking a scrawled, blurry star that another street kid from the market had tattooed onto his skin using the tip of a wood splinter and a match. Then he went on. One morning as he was sleeping off a high in the dirt beneath a market stand, he was awakened by a man. "*Hijo,*" he said, "*soy tu padre.*" Son, I'm your father. He'd never seen the man before and wondered for a second if he was so wasted that he couldn't even recognize his own father. But no, he was sure he'd never seen the man before. "You're not my father," he said, "I don't know you." The stranger replied: "I'm a son of God. You're a son of God. So I'm your father even if we've never met. Are you hungry? Come with me, I know a place where you'll find a bed, enough to eat, and real friends." The man took Segundo to a safe house, a church facility that tried to help street kids improve their lives. But Segundo's first attempt was a failure. After a few weeks, he ran away again and took up his old life right where he'd left off. Only it was much worse. He robbed, stole, and fought like he was out of his mind. On the street, he now called himself "Seyhau," which was how he pronounced "safe house." Then he tried to steal a purse that turned out to belong to the wrong woman, because her son beat him almost to death. He lay in the dirt for weeks, living off garbage from the market and thinking about suicide. One day just after he'd turned sixteen, he tried to stab himself in the stomach with a broken bottle. A quiet internal voice that he'd never heard before caused him to hesitate. He gripped the bottle so tightly that it broke—if you've ever handled one of those thin glass bottles from the jungle, you know this is possible. He fell asleep crying. After a long time, when he was finally back on his feet, he stole a fish from a market stand out of desperation. But this time he had even worse luck: The police saw him do it and came after him. They had no trouble catching him, of course—in his condition, even a turtle could have overtaken him. One of the cops stabbed him in the chest with a pointed, spear-like object, just barely missing his heart. He fell to the ground screaming, with blood shooting out of the wound. The market people egged the police on: "Kill him, kill him!" He whined, begged for help, swore he would change his life. Then he lost consciousness. At this point in his story, Segundo stopped and stared at the river for a second, then continued. Up until that moment he'd never thought about God. But as he lay there with darkness all around him, he heard a voice. It was the same voice he'd heard when he'd tried to kill himself. It said: "Segundo, what are you doing with your life? Do you really want to die like this?" He answered: "No, I'm not ready to die. But I don't want to live anymore, either." The voice said, "Then do it differently this time." All of a sudden he got his breath back; he said the feeling was like surfacing from a black sea. When he opened his eyes, he was staring into a cool hospital light. Someone had dumped him there. Even though he was safe in the hospital, Segundo was still afraid. The hospital bed cost a lot of money, and he didn't have a cent. A sympathetic head doctor let him leave without paying, and Segundo dragged himself to the safe house with his freshly bandaged wound. He swore that this time he would do better. The priest took him in. At first Segundo spent most of his time sleeping, talked very little, and cried a lot. Then he went to church for the first time.

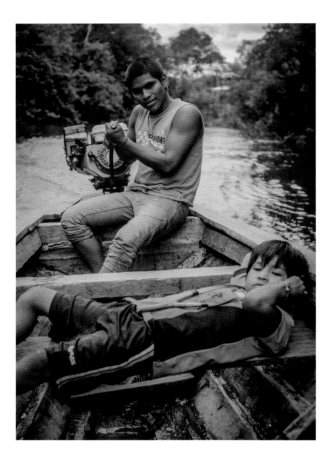

Churches in Peru are nothing like the magnificent, cold, incense-impregnated monuments we have in Germany. There, a church is a simple, unadorned building that could second as a school gym. People meet there on weekends to dance, sing, and pray, often until dawn. Segundo had found a new home and a new family. He read the Bible and applied its parables to his life. It was his support, and for him it seemed to work. He spoke so convincingly that even I, a hard-core atheist, listened closely as he quoted Bible verses and talked intelligently about his inner struggle to live a more positive life. Only a person who's learned his lessons the hard way can tell his story so reflectively. We were truly impressed. Once Segundo had found some inner stability, he tackled his next big challenge, but this time it ended well. He knocked on his mother's door and was able to reconcile with her. But he still hadn't managed to free himself from alcoholism or join the church. Looking determined, Segundo swore that he'd never give up on his goals. His uncle adopted him as a second son and gave him a job, the first honest money Segundo had ever earned. It felt damn good, he said. He laughed, and quickly wiped a tear from the corner of his eye. His new job: captain of a boat. His uncle's name: Edwin.

O ur time in the jungle was coming to an end. As a parting gift, we gave Edwin photos of our jungle tour that we'd had developed. He could use them to advertise his tours. To Segundo we gave an English text-book, something he'd been saving up to buy for a long time. The two saw us off with tears in their eyes. What fantastic people! One last time, we ate *anticuchos* and yucca empanadas in the streets of Iquitos, and then caught our flight to Cusco.

Cusco is the former capital of the Incan empire. From there we made our way to the ruined city of Machu Picchu. There are several ways to ascend Machu Picchu Mountain to reach the ruins. We chose to go by train. The tracks ran along bottomless inclines, finally reaching an altitude of around 6,500 feet (2,000 meters). Even higher mountains towered on either side. The Incan city was itself impressive and the view was incredible and vast. If only you could get rid of the hordes of buses full of package tourists! Everyone was taking the same souvenir photo. Mass production was not our cup of tea, so we beat an inconspicuous retreat. We still had to get back to Cusco and experience the classic Peruvian guinea pig dish called *cuy*. We tried it several times, always hoping that the next time we'd like it but, honestly, it's nothing to write home about. All bones—guinea pigs have almost no meat.

After a week of breathing thin, cold, high-altitude air, we were ready for a change, so we made our way to the south Peruvian desert and Arequipa, also known as the "White City." We arrived with a particular mission in mind: We'd heard of a traditional Peruvian dish called *pachamanca*. The Peruvians heat rocks in a fire pit, lay meat and vegetables on top, and then seal it all up with bunches of herbs and dirt. A few hours later, they dig up a fully cooked, extremely juicy meal. We planned to make this dish using a lamb we'd slaughtered ourselves. We'd always wanted to have this experience in order to broaden our perspective on meat consumption.

For every steak, an animal dies, and we need to be aware of that. Which is why we wanted to look the reality of our meat consumption right in the face, including killing the animal ourselves. In European culture, animals are almost always slaughtered behind closed doors in meat-processing plants. This makes it easier for people to enjoy their plates full of meat without ever coming into contact with the dirty business of slaughtering and butchering. Although the story we're about to tell may seem brutal, we recommend that you keep reading. It changed our view of meat eating forever.

KILLING IN THE NAME OF

At a restaurant in Arequipa, we asked if there was someplace in the area that we could get traditional *pachamanca*. We were sent to Don Beto, who ran a *pachamanca* restaurant just outside the city. As we talked to Don Beto about *pachamanca*, we also explained our intention: We wanted to experience for ourselves what it felt like to slaughter, skin, dress, and cut up a mammal for food. He invited us to his *pachamanca* grill.

The next morning, we took a taxi to Don Beto's place on the outskirts of Arequipa. It was sunny and still cool. There was dew on the grass in front of his house—nights in the desert are as freezing cold as the days are hot. A lamb was tied to a small olive tree and grazing peacefully. Don Beto offered us breakfast and coffee, because you shouldn't slaughter on an empty stomach. He'd gotten the lamb from a butcher friend of his who had also come along for the slaughter. Even though we were willing to do it ourselves, he explained, the lamb had to be killed instantly with a single, deliberate cut and that required a lot of experience. If you didn't cut through the spot on the larynx at exactly the right angle, the animal suffered. But we could do everything else, including skinning, dressing, and cutting it up. He had good reasons for wanting to do the actual slaughtering himself, so we agreed. While the others were still drinking coffee, I went alone to visit the lamb under the olive tree. When it saw me, it briefly raised its head as though it were thinking and then went back to grazing. I ran my hands over its wool. It was completely unafraid and sniffed me inquiringly, tugging at my pants pocket with its lips. My conscience was starting to nag me. It was a terrible feeling to know that this unsuspecting lamb was about to die because of me. I untied it and stroked its head. The others were now approaching from the house. Things were about to get serious.

I led the lamb to a small pit in the garden. As we stood there, it suddenly comprehended exactly what this was all about. It struggled so hard, it took all my strength just to hold onto it and keep it from running away. When the lamb realized that I was too strong for it, it immediately gave up, baa-ing softly, and its entire body started to tremble. I realized where we got the term "sacrificial lamb": This animal was surrendering without a fight.

The butcher took the lamb from me, grabbed it by the legs, and threw it to the ground. He kneeled with one leg over the lamb's body. With one hand he grabbed it by the scruff of the neck and pulled back its head. And then everything happened in a flash: Within two seconds he'd completely severed the lamb's head. Now I understood what he meant by a "tricky cut." He'd run the knife across the throat and behind the ears in a slight arc and cut through the cartilage of the spinal column as though it were butter. Blood from the lamb's throat spurted more than a foot (almost a half a meter). He inserted a stick in the windpipe. The lamb's body continued to jerk for several minutes, its legs moving as if trotting. It moved for so long that we had a hard time believing it was really dead, but its head was lying about 3 feet (1 meter) away. Finally it gave up the ghost and its body lay motionless on the ground. The blood ran dry. Now it was our turn. We cut open the belly and removed the innards.

We then lifted the body onto a steel table and started to skin it. First we cut the tendons at the knee joints and broke off the lower legs with a single snap. They weren't needed anymore. We grasped the hide and, starting at the belly, carefully separated it from the body using a sharp knife. We had to pull extremely hard to loosen it from the muscle. Once the lamb was dressed and skinned, an amazing thing happened: The animal became meat. Without its head, hide, or hooves, what had formerly been a living creature suddenly became—in our conscious minds—food.

We transferred the dressed lamb to a tub of water and washed it inside and out. Then, with expert cuts, we quickly reduced it to individual pieces. That's a standard part of meat preparation, so we'd had lots of practice. We then marinated it and placed it in Don Beto's pit of hot stones. Mission accomplished.

So what did we learn? If everybody had to butcher their own meat, there would definitely be a lot more vegetarians in the world. Meat on the plate looks very different when you've killed the animal yourself. The experience of slaughtering was different from anything we'd ever known before. We felt gratitude and appreciation for the lamb. And a little guilt. Killing just feels wrong.

IN PERU, PACHAMANCA IS AN EVENT FOR THE WHOLE FAMILY. THEY ALL PITCH IN, TREAT THEMSELVES TO LOTS OF BEER AND COCA LEAF LIQUEUR, AND CELEBRATE ALL DAY LONG.

PACHAMANCA
PIT-ROASTED LAMB

No, we don't have a fire pit in our backyard, but cooking *pachamanca* in a roasting pan is as close as you can get to the real thing.

SERVES 6

1 CUP FRESH TARRAGON

½ CUP FRESH THYME

½ CUP OREGANO

1 TEASPOON WHOLE BLACK PEPPERCORNS

1 TEASPOON COARSE SEA SALT

6 TABLESPOONS OLIVE OIL

2¼ TO 3⅓ POUNDS (1 TO 1.5 KG) LAMB SHANK OR BONE-IN LAMB SHOULDER

1 (3-POUND) WHOLE CHICKEN, PREFERABLY ORGANIC, CLEANED, CUT INTO 4 TO 6 PIECES

1⅔ POUNDS SWEET POTATOES

1 CUP FAVA BEANS

2 EARS CORN

5 CLOVES GARLIC

FRESHLY GROUND BLACK PEPPER

2 LARGE YELLOW ONIONS, QUARTERED

½ CUP (120 ML) RED WINE VINEGAR

Place the tarragon, thyme, oregano, peppercorns, salt, and 3 tablespoons of the olive oil in a blender and purée until a paste forms. Rub this paste into the lamb shank and all over the chicken. Marinate both in the refrigerator for 1 hour.

Preheat the oven to 300°F (150°C). Clean and quarter the sweet potatoes, leaving on the skin. Clean the fava beans and ears of corn. Cut the corn into thirds, so you have 6 pieces. Peel the garlic cloves.

Place the sweet potatoes, fava beans, and corn in a very large roasting pan with a lid. Pour the remaining 3 tablespoons olive oil over the top and season with lots of salt and pepper. Put the lamb and chicken, including the marinade, into the pan, cover it, and bake for 3 to 3½ hours.

Meanwhile, place the onion quarters in a bowl and pour the vinegar over the top. Mix together well, cover, and put the onions in the refrigerator.

Increase the oven temperature to broil and remove the lid from the roasting pan. Broil the meat for about 7 minutes per side, for a total of about 15 minutes, or until a nice crust has formed.

Remove the lamb and chicken from the roasting pan. Distribute the sweet potatoes, beans, and corn on each plate, add a piece of chicken and lamb to each, and pour the liquid from the roasting pan over the meat. Top with the onions marinated in vinegar.

You must eat this with your hands

Our last stop in Peru took us once again to a deserted beach. Punta Bombón: surfing, grilling fish over a campfire, and saying farewell to the Peruvian ocean. Of course, you can also make this dish on a regular grill, but it's more awesome to grill it on a stick set over a fire. All you really need to prepare it is a knife and a cutting board. But driftwood works, too.

FISH WITH VEGETABLE PACKETS

SERVES 2

VEGETABLE PACKETS

2 FRESH FIGS

1 TOMATO

1 LARGE SWEET POTATO

1 MEDIUM RED ONION

1 RED THAI CHILE PEPPER

1 LIME

½ CUP GREEN OR BLACK OLIVES

5 OUNCES FETA CHEESE

1 BUNCH CILANTRO, TORN INTO SMALL PIECES

4 CLOVES GARLIC

SALT AND FRESHLY GROUND BLACK PEPPER

FISH

1 (5-OUNCE) WHOLE BONITO FISH,
(OR ANOTHER FIRM FISH)

2 TABLESPOONS OLIVE OIL

SALT AND FRESHLY GROUND BLACK PEPPER

1 LIME

VARIOUS FRESH HERBS (SUCH AS PARSLEY,
ROSEMARY, BASIL—WHATEVER YOU CAN GET)

2 CLOVES GARLIC

Light your campfire! Or if at home, prepare a grill to cook at medium heat.

Prepare all of the ingredients for the vegetable packets: Halve the figs. Cut the tomato into eighths. Peel and dice the sweet potato. Peel and quarter the onion. Cut the chile pepper in half and remove the seeds. Slice the lime into eighths.

Lay out two 10-inch (25 cm) sheets of aluminum foil and pile the prepared vegetables and olives in the center of each square. Crumble a little feta on top. Divide the cilantro pieces between the packets, and add 2 cloves of garlic to each packet. Season with salt and pepper to taste. Fold all four corners of the foil toward the center and twist them together to make sealed vegetable packets. Place the packets on the coals of your fire. They will need to cook for about 30 minutes, depending on how hot your fire is. This gives the mixture plenty of time to caramelize and develop a fantastic aroma.

While the vegetable packets are cooking, rub the fish inside and out with olive oil and season it with salt and pepper. Thinly slice the lime. Stuff the fish with lime slices, herbs, and garlic and fasten its belly closed with toothpicks. Shove two

forked sticks into the ground on either side of the fire and lay your stick holding the fish across them. Cook the fish for 10 to 12 minutes.

If you prepare the fish on a grill, place it in a roasting pan directly over the coals or use a fish grilling basket. Serve the fish with the vegetable packets, and enjoy.

GRILLING ON A STICK

1 LONG WOODEN STICK, THOROUGHLY SOAKED IN SEAWATER (YOU DON'T WANT IT TO BURN AND DROP YOUR FISH INTO THE FIRE)
2 STICKS FORKED ON ONE END

Sharpen one end of the long stick and insert it into the fish's mouth. Carefully slide the fish onto the stick until the tip reaches the fish's belly. Continue forcing the stick through the back third of the fish until it comes out at the tailfin. Do this slowly and carefully to keep from doing too much damage to the fish. If you have any wire handy, wrap a little around the fish to ensure that it stays firmly fastened to the stick.

AJÍ DE GALLINA

PERUVIAN-STYLE
CHICKEN FRICASSEE

SERVES 1

2 STALKS CELERY
1 CARROT, PEELED
½ LEEK
3 CLOVES GARLIC, PEELED
1 (8-OUNCE) SKINLESS CHICKEN BREAST
6 AJÍ AMARILLO (LONG YELLOW PERUVIAN CHILE PEPPERS) OR 3 YELLOW BELL PEPPERS
2 AJÍ MIRASOL (DRIED AJÍ AMARILLO) OR DRIED YELLOW OR RED BELL PEPPERS

1 PIECE WHITE BREAD, TOASTED
5 PECANS OR WALNUTS
1 TABLESPOON OLIVE OIL
½ MEDIUM WHITE ONION, DICED
⅔ CUP (160 ML) MILK
10 PITTED BLACK OLIVES, FINELY CHOPPED
SALT AND FRESHLY GROUND BLACK PEPPER
SLICED COOKED POTATOES OR COOKED WHITE RICE, FOR SERVING

Remove the seeds from the fresh and dried yellow chile peppers. In a second pot of simmering water, simmer the peppers for 3 minutes. Remove them and let them cool slightly. Repeat these steps two more times. This reduces the peppers' spiciness while bringing out their fantastic fruity aroma. If you use yellow bell peppers, simply simmer them for 6 minutes total, or until tender.

Purée the chile (or bell) peppers with a little of the chicken stock and the remaining 2 cloves garlic to make a smooth, bright yellow sauce.

Soak the toast in 1 cup of the stock to soften, and purée the toast, stock, and nuts to make a uniformly thick and creamy mixture. This will be your sauce thickener.

Heat the olive oil in a pot and sauté the onion for 10 to 12 minutes, until translucent. Add the chile pepper sauce to the pot and simmer over low heat for 15 minutes, or until the sauce has thickened slightly and becomes fragrant. At the very end, stir in a little olive oil to make the sauce a little creamier. Add your homemade sauce thickener and simmer for another few minutes.

Cut the chicken breast into cubes. Add the chicken, milk, and olives to the pot and simmer for a few more minutes. Season the fricassee with salt and pepper to taste. You can serve this fricassee over cooked potato slices or with rice.

SEE VIDEO:

Arica   Iquique

SANTIAGO

Pichilemu

Chile: the world's longest country, stretching 2,671 miles (4,300 kilometers) from its northernmost tip to Patagonia in the south. Apart from Antarctica, Patagonia is the southernmost point in the world. That's were we wanted to be! In the north, the climate is mild and Mediterranean-like. In the south, it's a little harsher, the wind is always blowing, and it's bitter cold.

We found Chileans to be sincere, friendly people. Chile has a lot fewer problems with corruption and drugs than the Latin American countries farther north. We had just under a month to take in as much as possible, so we plunged right in.

Pichilemu
Puntilla
Punta de lobos
Torres del Paine
PUNTA ARENAS
PUERTO NATALES

Our journey through Chile started in the far north, at the surf spots in Arica and Iquique. But all the waves were small, and there wasn't much to do generally, so we didn't stay long. Instead we continued on to Santiago de Chile, where our Chilean friend Jean-Paul and his relatives were expecting us. Our host family, the Naudóns, was famous in the district for their butchering skills. They served up huge, carnivorous feasts that took some getting used to, especially after our *pachamanca* experience in Peru (see page 278).

Here, the South American stereotype held true: The entire extended family was scurrying around the house. On Sundays, they set up a gigantic table in the garden. The uncles all stood around a huge grill, holding bottles of beer and turning twenty steaks and just as many chicken leg quarters, chops, and more. Meanwhile, the mamas and grandmas were in the kitchen preparing *pebre*, a typical Chilean sauce that no meal is complete without, as well as salads and side dishes. Once everything had been stirred, grilled, chopped, and cooked, we all sat down at the table

to eat. The conversation was rarely civil—more often, they would single out one person to pick on. Then everybody, from the sweet little grandkids to the old grandpa, would go after the poor jerk and be doubled over with laughter. Cozy was wise enough to sit at the end of the table, where he laughed politely and claimed not to understand a thing. So who do you think the spotlight settled on? Me, of course, sitting toward the middle of the table, wedged between the fat uncles. I don't know what set it off; I didn't understand what they were saying. I think I may have held a chicken leg the wrong way, or something like that. In any case, I was fair game. The Chileans twisted around every gesture I made, every word I spoke, until they ended up referring to me as either a lady-boy or a little princess in a pink tutu. How did we get there? To hell with my knowledge of Spanish—I didn't understand a word of this Chilean pidgin! I never stood a chance. Fortunately there was plenty of beer and schnapps, and after what felt like way too long, the woman of the house finally took my side and spoke a few choice words in my defense. At last I was allowed to sit back, relax, and enjoy the show.

CARNE À LA NAUDÓN
CHILEAN TRIPE STEW

Chileans also add white bread soaked in milk to this stew during cooking to thicken. Try it sometime—it's really delicious!

SERVES 4

OLIVE OIL, FOR FRYING

1½ POUNDS (700 G) PREPARED (COOKED) VEAL TRIPE, CUT INTO STRIPS (IF USING RAW TRIPE, SEE COOK'S NOTE BELOW)

2 CLOVES GARLIC, FINELY CHOPPED

1 RED CHILE, SEEDED AND MINCED

SALT AND FRESHLY GROUND BLACK PEPPER

2 LARGE YELLOW ONIONS, SLICED INTO RINGS

⅓ CUP (80 ML) DRY RED WINE

4¼ CUPS (1 LITER) BEEF STOCK

2 LARGE TOMATOES

2½ POUNDS POTATOES, COOKED

HANDFUL OF WALNUTS, COARSELY CHOPPED

2 TABLESPOONS DRIED MARJORAM

2 TABLESPOONS DRIED OREGANO

2-OUNCE (60 G) BLOCK OF PARMESAN

HANDFUL OF FRESH BASIL LEAVES, FOR GARNISH

In a large, high-sided pan, heat the oil over medium heat and sauté the tripe with the garlic and chile. Season it well with salt and pepper. Add the onions and continue frying for 5 more minutes. Be careful that it doesn't burn! Pour in the red wine, continue simmering for 3 minutes, and then add the beef stock. Cover the pan and simmer the stew for 10 minutes.

Cut the tomatoes into eighths. Cut the potatoes into bite-size pieces. Add the tomatoes, potatoes, walnuts, marjoram, and oregano to the stew and stir it well. Simmer the stew for another 5 minutes. While stirring, gradually grate in the cheese until the stew has a creamy consistency.

Serve the stew in soup bowls, garnished with fresh basil and seasoned with pepper to taste. Enjoy!

COOK'S NOTE: IF YOU CAN ONLY FIND RAW VEAL TRIPE, SIMPLY RINSE THE TRIPE UNDER COOL WATER TO RID THE TRIPE OF ANY BLOOD OR CLEANING SOLUTION THAT THE BUTCHER USES. THE TRIPE IS CLEAN WHEN IT IS WHITE WITH NO TRACES OF BLOODY RESIDUE. PLACE THE TRIPE IN A LARGE STOCKPOT AND FILL THE STOCKPOT ¾ FULL WITH WATER. BRING THE TRIPE AND WATER TO A BOIL OVER HIGH HEAT. REDUCE THE HEAT TO MEDIUM, COVER THE POT AND SIMMER THE TRIPE FOR 1 HOUR.

The butcher family took us in and treated us like their own sons. But when we weighed ourselves at the end of a week, it was clear that we had to move on as soon as possible. We'd had a message on our Facebook page from two Chilean surfers, Claudio and Fabio, who invited us to Pichilemu, where they were renting a couple cabanas on the beach and surfing every day. When we learned that one of them was also an excellent chef who had trained in kitchens throughout Latin America, we knew exactly where we had to go. For the last time on this trip, we tied our surfboards onto the roof of the rental car and took off.

We had to drive around for a while before finding the address the guys had given us. To make it easier for you: Las Acacias 620, Infiernillo, Pichilemu. Our time there was awesome. The days with Claudio were as instructive as all the rest of the trip put together. This chapter contains a special section devoted to Claudio's best recipes. He also taught us the most interesting ceviche recipe that we'd ever tasted. He'd spent some time working in a first-class restaurant on Easter Island, among other places, which is how he ended up combining Polynesian South Seas cuisine with traditional Peruvian-style ceviche: fish, lime, onions, coconut milk, mango, chile, ginger, cilantro, cucumber...you've got to try it! We organized a beach party with Claudio and Fabio beside a small, hidden bay. There wasn't another soul in sight. We cooked fresh fish and a fruit-and-vegetable dish on the beach and surfed. Anyone visiting Chile who wants to be by the ocean should rent a cabana like Claudio and Fabio: Cabañas Infiernillo is where it's at!

CLAUDIO'S POLYNESIAN CEVICHE

When preparing this ceviche, it's extremely important that you follow the steps in the proper order. Throughout the process, the fish must stay cold, which is why Claudio first puts a handful of ice cubes in the bowl he uses to make it.

SERVES 4

2¼ POUNDS (1 KG) SUSHI-QUALITY WHITE FISH, SUCH AS SOLE OR SEA BASS (IN OTHER WORDS, SOMETHING CLASSY)

HANDFUL OF ICE CUBES

1 LARGE RED ONION

1 SCALLION, GREEN PART ONLY

½ CUCUMBER

1 RED BANANA CHILE

1 MANGO

1 TABLESPOON SESAME SEEDS

1 CHILE PEPPER, SEEDED AND MINCED

⅓ INCH (1 CM) FRESH GINGER, GRATED

1 BUNCH CILANTRO, COARSELY CHOPPED

ZEST AND JUICE OF 2 LEMONS

¼ CUP VEGETABLE OIL

JUICE OF 6 LIMES

1⅔ CUPS (400 ML) UNSWEETENED COCONUT MILK

SALT AND FRESHLY GROUND BLACK PEPPER

Cut the fish into ⅓-inch (1 cm) cubes and place it in a bowl along with the ice cubes.

Remove the fish from the bowl of ice, pat dry and place in a clean bowl. Remove the two or three outermost layers from the onion and slice the inner layers into thin rings. Cut the scallion green into thin rings. Peel the cucumber and cut it into slices ¼ inch (5 mm) thick. Cut the banana pepper into thin strips. Peel the mango and cut the flesh into ⅓-inch (1 cm) cubes. Toast the sesame seeds in a dry skillet over low heat.

After removing the ice and draining the fish cubes, add all of the above ingredients to the fish, along with the chile pepper, ginger, cilantro, and lemon zest, and toss them with the oil. The fish will soak up all the aromas like a sponge and become saturated with oil.

Finally, add the lime and lemon juices and the coconut milk, stir well, and transfer the ceviche to a large salad bowl or casserole dish. As a finishing touch, Claudio sprinkles more toasted sesame seeds and cilantro over the top, and then it's ready to eat.

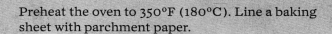

CLAUDIO'S STUFFED FISH

WITH FRIED CHORIZO AND CHICKPEA-PAPAYA SALAD

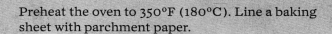

SERVES 4

3 STALKS LEMONGRASS
1 BUNCH CILANTRO
2 FRESH RED CHILES
4 CLOVES GARLIC
4 (1-POUND) WHOLE FISH
(SUCH AS SEA BREAM, SEA BASS,
TROUT, OR RED SNAPPER), CLEANED
1 LEMON, CUT INTO SLICES
1 LIME, CUT INTO SLICES
SEVERAL SPRIGS THAI BASIL
OLIVE OIL, FOR COOKING
3 TABLESPOONS WHITE WINE
1²/₃ POUNDS (750 G) RAW CHORIZO SAUSAGES
3¹/₂ CUPS (500 G) DICED PAPAYA
1¹/₃ CUPS (200 G) GREEN GRAPES, HALVED
1 (15-OUNCE/450 G) CAN CHICKPEAS, DRAINED
JUICE OF 1 LIME
SALT AND FRESHLY GROUND BLACK PEPPER

Preheat the oven to 350°F (180°C). Line a baking sheet with parchment paper.

Cut open the lemongrass stalks lengthwise. Set aside several cilantro sprigs and chop the rest. Remove the seeds from the chiles. Chop one chile very finely and quarter the other. Peel the garlic and crush it slightly with a heavy knife handle.

Rinse the fish well, pat dry with paper towels, and fill the cavities with lemon and lime slices, lemongrass, cilantro, Thai basil, the quarted chile pepper, and the garlic cloves.

Lay the fish on the prepared baking sheet, drizzle them with a little oil and white wine, and cook them in the oven for 25 to 35 minutes. The time will vary depending on the size of the fish, but make sure you don't leave them in the oven for too long or they'll dry out. Toward the end of the cooking time, turn the oven temperature to broil. Broil the fish for 5 minutes, or until they're nice and crispy.

Heat a little oil in a skillet, and brown the whole chorizos on all sides for about 10 minutes; it's okay if they get a little burnt! When cool enough to handle, slice the sausages.

Chop the reserved cilantro sprigs. Combine the chopped cilantro, papaya, grapes, chickpeas, lime juice, and chopped chile in a bowl, mix thoroughly, and season with salt and pepper to taste.

Serve the fish with sliced chorizo and the chickpea salad. You can put the sausage directly on top of the fish, if you like. Its powerful juices mix with the fine aromas of the fish—a combination you don't want to miss!

CLAUDIO'S MUSSEL SOUP

SERVES 6

2 MEDIUM YELLOW ONIONS
4 CLOVES GARLIC
OLIVE OIL
1 CUP (240 ML) DRY WHITE WINE
2 CUPS (480 ML) FISH STOCK,
STORE-BOUGHT OR HOMEMADE (PAGE 302)
1¾ CUPS (450 G) CHOPPED TOMATOES,
WITH JUICES
SALT AND FRESHLY GROUND BLACK PEPPER
1⅛ POUNDS (500 G) MUSSELS
2¼ POUNDS (1 KG) CLAMS
(YOU CAN SUBSTITUTE ANOTHER
TYPE OF SHELLFISH IF YOU WANT)
1 BUNCH CILANTRO, CHOPPED
1 BUNCH PARSLEY, CHOPPED

Peel the onions and garlic cloves and dice both. Heat a little olive oil in a very large pot or wok and sauté the onions and garlic over medium heat for several minutes. Pour in the white wine and simmer the mixture for 5 minutes to evaporate the alcohol. Then add the fish stock and tomatoes and stir everything together carefully. Season with salt and pepper to taste.

Rinse all the mussels and clams thoroughly in a large colander and add them to the stock. Stir them all once and then cover the pot! This is very important because the steam produced ensures that all the mussels and clams are cooked evenly and not just the ones that are under water! Simmer the shellfish for 5 to 8 minutes.

As soon as the mussels and clams have opened, remove the pot from the heat and sprinkle them with cilantro and parsley, discarding any mussels and clams that are still closed. Drizzle olive oil over the mussels and clams and stir them well—and start eating immediately! It's best to eat the mussels and clams with your hands, right out of the pot. You'll have fewer dishes to wash and you'll have more fun.

FISH STOCK

MAKES 8⅓ CUPS (2 LITERS)

2 LARGE YELLOW ONIONS
1 LARGE TOMATO
2 STALKS CELERY
½ FENNEL BULB
2 CARROTS
5 CLOVES GARLIC
2 TABLESPOONS UNSALTED BUTTER
3⅓ POUNDS (1.5 KG) FISH BONES
4¼ CUPS (1 LITER) WHITE WINE
1 SPRIG ROSEMARY
1 SPRIG THYME
3 BAY LEAVES
10 WHOLE BLACK PEPPERCORNS
2 WHOLE CLOVES
1 TABLESPOON SALT

Peel and halve the onions. Halve the tomato. Cut the celery and fennel into large pieces. Peel the carrots and cut them into large pieces as well. Peel the garlic and crush it slightly with a heavy knife handle.

Melt the butter in a large pot over low heat. Sauté the fish bones for several minutes so that they develop a strong aroma. Then pour the white wine and 8⅓ cups (2 liters) water over the bones and add the rosemary, thyme, bay leaves, peppercorns, cloves, and salt. Cover the pot and simmer for at least 45 minutes. The longer you simmer the stock, the more flavor it will develop, but 2 hours should be plenty.

Strain the stock through a fine-mesh strainer into a bowl, return it to the pot, and simmer it for another 20 minutes, uncovered, to reduce it by about one-quarter. This gives the stock an even more intense and concentrated flavor. You'll smell it—unbeatable!

MELVIN

Melvin—it's a combination of melon and vino, which should already give you a hint about what it's going to be....Depending on your level of hunger and thirst, this can serve 2 to 4 people.

1 MEDIUM CANTALOUPE OR HONEYDEW MELON
1 (750 ML) BOTTLE DRY WHITE WINE OR PROSECCO

Cut the top off the melon and a small bit on the base of the melon to make a flat surface, then remove all the seeds with a spoon.

Once you've removed all the seeds, keep scraping until about 2 inches (5 centimeters) of flesh and melon juice have accumulated in the bottom.

Top off the melon with the white wine and stir it once.

Done! Naturally, this tastes best when the temperature outside is 85°F (30°C).

CHILE SURF GUIDE

ARICA

EL TUBO -18.45291°N -70.30701°E

El Tubo is right on the main beach where a pier once stood, as you can see by the iron bars sticking out of the water. Despite its promising name, it's more of a beginner beach break with a few peaks. With a southwest to northwest swell, it's doable, and it's best at high tide. If it's more than 6½ feet (2 meters), all you get are closeouts.

IQUIQUE

PUNTA DOS -20.22588°N -70.15208°E

Punta Dos is a wicked hollow tube that breaks over a sharp reef. The wave is absolutely unforgiving and only for experienced surfers. Your takeoff has to be extremely fast and you need to get out of the wave early enough to avoid being rolled over the sharp, sea urchin–covered reef. Mainly rights but, depending on the swell, there's also the occasional left. The spot is under the firm control of the local bodyboarder community, so it isn't easy to get a good wave. I caught a couple of nice tubes here, but I had to take huge risks to beat out all the bodyboarders. At the end of the session I probably took too big a risk, as evidenced by the deep 2-inch (5 cm) scar above my hip.

PICHILEMU

In the Indian language, *Pichilemu* means "little forest." This surfer paradise is located about 160 miles (260 kilometers) south of Santiago de Chile and is famous for the consistency and quality of its waves. This guide was written for us by Fabio, one of two surfers who invited us to their homes.

The prevailing climate at Pichilemu is Mediterranean, but the water gets down to 53°F (12°C) in the winter. (Important: Winter in Chile is summer in the Northern Hemisphere.) So it's highly recommended that you wear a 4/3 wetsuit and boots in winter. In the summer a 3/2 wetsuit is sufficient. Pichilemu is located in a picturesque area surrounded by steep, rocky cliffs, sandy beaches, and rambling pine groves, so it appeals to nature lovers as well as surfers.

There's a wide range of accommodations and restaurants available with a good selection of fresh fish and seafood dishes. After surfing in the cold water, it's the ideal place to refuel!

Above all, Pichilemu is known for these two bays with their left-hand point breaks:

PUNTILLA -34.38058°N -72.01566°E

This surf spot is located at the southern tip of Pichilemu's main beach, where there's also a large observation deck with a view of the surf. Go through a channel between some rocks and you can paddle directly out to the peak. The wave itself breaks over a sandbank.

This left breaks all year long—sometimes bigger, sometimes smaller. Depending on the season and the swell, its shape varies from powerful, heavy barrels to pleasant beginner waves. In the summer, there are usually tons of surfers in the water, and it's recommended that you get there as early in the day as possible so you'll have a little less competition in the lineup. It's best to visit Pichilemu during the off-season, in April or November. Then you'll only have to share the wave with a few friendly locals.

PUNTA DE LOBOS -34.42528°N -72.04275°E

About 3¾ miles (6 kilometers) south of Pichilemu is the
Punta de Lobos nature reserve, formerly known as a natural habitat for large numbers of sea lions, which even
today can pop up in the lineup now and then. This is where
the biggest and most famous wave in the region breaks in
front of impressive, steep cliffs, one of which rises out
of the water like a mighty tower, right next to the main
peak. Punta de Lobos is a left-hand point break over sand.
The way to get there is very unusual and even legendary.
First you take a steep, narrow path down the cliffs to the
beach below. There you wait for the exact moment when
a wave is spilling over a mussel-encrusted reef to jump
from algae-covered rocks into the water. You then paddle through a small channel to a large bird cliff that juts
out of the sea like a tower. You pull yourself over seaweed
and onto the base of the cliff and balance on the other side
of the rock. When the next wave comes, you jump back
into the water and paddle with the current between a few
more boulders, wait for a short pause between sets, and,
one or two duck dives later, you're there. You'll be well
rewarded for your efforts—you'll find gigantic, deep-blue
barrels just waiting for you as the sun dips behind the bird
cliffs. Surfer porn!

WHAT, DECEMBER ALREADY?

Since we began our trip in Cuba, we'd been dreaming of the moment when we would have finished all our work and could stand in southern Patagonia looking out at the ocean, going over everything we'd experienced one more time. Now we were almost there. After surfing our last wave at Pichilemu, we caught a flight from Santiago to Punta Arenas in Patagonia, the far end of the continent. The approach to the airport was not for the faint-hearted. Even we, as world travelers with loads of flying experience, were scared shitless. Down there, at the end of the civilized world, a severe storm is always raging. You could already see it from an altitude of 3,280 feet (1,000 meters), how the gusts were raising up the otherwise flat ocean

and carrying the spray umpteen feet across the surface. The plane waggled like a cow's tail in a swarm of flies. We were flung left and right and, for the first time ever, we admitted that it might be a good idea to fasten our seatbelts. Please, let's not croak with only a few feet to go. All our work would be wasted and our book would never be published. But for the pilot, plunging practically headfirst toward a tiny airstrip seemed routine. Someone behind us barfed into a bag just two minutes before landing. But before anything worse could happen, with just a few little hops we set down on the runway more or less gently.

When we climbed out of the plane, the wind practically tore us off the steps. Jean-Paul, who'd come along with us, just laughed. He'd been there a few times already and knew what to expect. We stayed in Punta Arenas at the Hostal del Rey, where a friendly elderly woman welcomed us into her small cottage, whose decoration she'd really put her heart into. Jean-Paul's distant kinship secured us a special rate, so it cost us almost nothing to stay there.

The many colorful houses and the severe climate gave the town a slightly Scandinavian feel. We rented our last compact car and drove to Torres del Paine National Park, rolling across lush pastureland where wild guanacos— the animal from which we got domestic llamas—were

running free. We also saw rheas, giant birds similar to African ostriches, searching for food among the bushes. The park itself was breathtaking. The Torres del Paine, meaning the "towers of blue," are massive, jagged rock towers extending into the sky. At the foot of the mountain range there were turquoise-blue lakes where the wind was whipping up foot-high waves. At one point, the gravel road went so close to the lake that our car was almost swept away by the masses of water being thrown up by the wind. In Lago Grey, we found ice-blue glaciers, just like in *National Geographic*. This was maybe the most impressive landscape we'd seen yet. We stopped on a hill, intending to enjoy the view from the top. Easier said than done. We ended up crawling around on all fours, because if we'd stood up, the wind would have blown us away. A wind velocity of over 62 miles (100 kilometers) per hour? Here, that's just a balmy breeze! After spending the day in the park, we were hungry and discovered one final awesome dish: At a ranch belonging to the first settlers, who happened to be nineteenth-century German immigrants, we ate Patagonian lamb. The whole lamb was stretched out on an iron cross and roasted over a bonfire until it was crisp on the outside and buttery soft and juicy inside. It was served with beets, roasted potatoes, and a hearty Chilean Cabernet Sauvignon. A fitting last supper!

HOME TO MAMA

On the last day of our trip, we got up early and one more time ran along the gravel path from the hostel down to the sea. We stared silently at the water for half an hour. It wasn't until that moment that it finally hit home—the year, and therefore our journey, was at an end. After a year in Latin America, we had accumulated countless incredible experiences, five terabytes of photos and video material, a gazillion new friends from all over the world, and more than thirty more tattoos.

Now we were heading back to Germany, just in time to celebrate Christmas with the family. Christmas, Germany—they seemed absurdly remote. What then? Go back to our old jobs? We agreed: No way. We didn't yet know how the Salt & Silver project would develop, whether we would market our own salsa creations or open a taco stand. Or maybe a ceviche shop? We'd find something. In the words of Mel C: "It's just the beginning, it's not the end...." We'll be seeing you!

JO & COZY
DECEMBER 2014

INDEX

313

315

LOCATIONS

WAVES

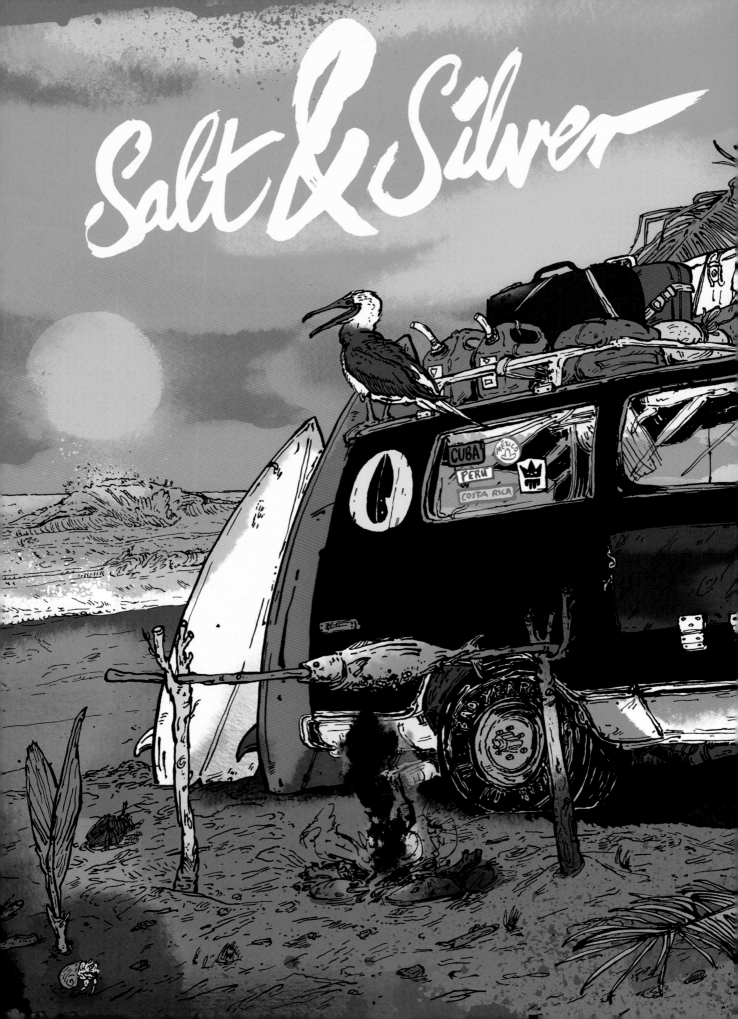

Jana Federov
MAPS & HANDWRITING
P. 8, 14, 16, 58, 60, 136, 138, 162, 164, 186, 188, 206, 208, 222, 230, 232, 290, 292

Kingdrips Fabian Wolf
www.kingdrips.com
RECIPE ICONS & ILLUSTRATIONS P. 13, 318, 319, ENDPAPERS

Paul Pack
PHOTO P. 6, 7

Tania Maia
ILLUSTRATIONS ON ENDPAPERS, P. 11, 12, 122

Ka Shim
PHOTO P. 21, BOTTOM

Kim Schröder & Antine Yzer
FOOD PHOTOGRAPHY
P. 22, 42, 50–55, 64, 72–79 , 129, 131, 153, 154, 263–265

Erick Cuevas
TATTOO FLASHES P. 80–83

Moisés Jiménez
TATTOO FLASHES P. 205

Chris Bailey
PHOTO P. 242

Daniela Garreton
ILLUSTRATION ON ENDPAPERS, LOWER LEFT-HAND CORNER

Enrique Rodriguez
PHOTO P. 241

Albert Ibáñez Nómad-A Media
PHOTO P. 226 BOTTOM

Nils Poppe, Dominik Gauly, Yulia Morozova
GRAPHIC DESIGN

Johannes Riffelmacher
ART DIRECTION

Johannes Riffelmacher
COVER ILLUSTRATION & LOGO DESIGN

Thomas Kosikowski & Johannes Riffelmacher
ALL OTHER PHOTOS, TEXTS, RECIPES

Andrews McMeel Publishing
a division of Andrews McMeel Universal
1130 Walnut Street, Kansas City, Missouri 64106
www.andrewsmcmeel.com

First published in 2015, © 2015 Neuer Umschau Buchverlag, Neustadt an der Weinstrasse.

16 17 18 19 20 21 TEN 10 9 8 7 6 5 4 3 2 1

ISBN: 978-1-4494-7121-7

Library of Congress Catalog Number: 2015955851

Christie Tam
ENGLISH TRANSLATION

Patty Holden
ENGLISH PRODUCTION

Laura Kirschbacher, Neustadt an der Weinstraße
EDITOR, READER

Birgit van der Avoort, Havixbeck
RECIPE READER

Blaschke Vision, Laubach
REPRO

ANDREWS MCMEEL PUBLISHING
Editor: Jean Z. Lucas
Art director: Holly Ogden
Copy chief: Maureen Sullivan
Production manager: Carol Coe
Demand planner: Sue Eikos

ATTENTION: SCHOOLS AND BUSINESSES
Andrews McMeel books are available at quantity discounts with bulk purchase for educational, business, or sales promotional use. For information, please e-mail the Andrews McMeel Publishing Special Sales Department:
specialsales@amuniversal.com.

to the
SEA